ROGER ZELAZNY'S VISUAL GUIDE TO CASTLE AMBER

Will—

ROGER ZELAZNY'S
V I S U A L
G U I D E   T O
CASTLE
AMBER

WRITTEN BY
ROGER ZELAZNY
& NEIL RANDALL
PAINTINGS BY
TODD CAMERON HAMILTON
MAPS BY
JAMES CLOUSE

AVON BOOKS
NEW YORK

ROGER ZELAZNY'S VISUAL GUIDE TO CASTLE AMBER is an original publication of Avon Books. This work has never before appeared in book form.

AVON BOOKS
A division of
The Hearst Corporation
1350 Avenue of the Americas
New York, New York 10019

CONTENTS

5

INTRODUCTION

We invaded his house. It's a simple as that.

For four days we occupied the peak hours of Roger Zelazny's day. Days when he should have been writing the ninth Amber novel. Or something about unicorns. Or cats. Or maybe even lords and light.

But he put up with us, all four of us. Todd Hamilton and Jim Clouse peppered him with question after interminable question about Castle Amber itself, and later about the art of the Trumps. Bill Fawcett, who organized it all, extracted even more information. I sat in the corner, reading the as-yet-unreleased *Sign of Chaos*. It was an honor, and I won't easily forget it.

And with each new question Roger Zelazny would stop, and raise his hands, and then put them back down and let the words pour forth. Often he would close his eyes as he talked, recalling every last detail about the world he created — or perhaps discovered — over the course of eight extremely popular novels. Sometimes he would hesitate, as if unwilling to tell us some Amberian secret, but in the end he would relent, and let us know what he was thinking about. Those thoughts — always — confirmed his belief in his world. Then we all began writing and drawing . . .

To read the artist's words is an unqualified privilege. But to watch an artist's mind at work — now there's something worth being alive to see.

To Roger Zelazny, our greatest thanks. For his help, for his hospitality, and for letting us watch him uncover the world he loves.

— Neil Randall
March 10th, 1988

ENTRANCE TO
CASTLE
AMBER

elcome to Castle Amber. I am your guide. I will accompany you as you journey through the castle, showing you the most important rooms and introducing you to anyone you should happen to meet. But before we begin, I must make a confession. I've lived a long time, and I've done a great many things. But never once have I been a tour guide.

Nor would I be now, but the King of Amber requested my expertise. Usually he asks the chief servants, sometimes one of the young princes. But Merlin is away right now, and Roger, the chief servant, has come down with pneumonia.

So, just this morning, Random summoned me. He asked me if I would act as tour guide for the visitors. He said I had the gift of speech, that I would render the visit more pleasant and more educational than it had ever been before. He said, too, that these visitors deserved the best. On all accounts, he was correct.

My name, by the way, is Flora. My title is Princess of Amber.

THE CASTLE EXTERIOR

Let's begin with a short walk outside, around the castle's perimeter. As you walked up from the harbor, you probably noticed two things. First, the castle is set in the side of a mountain. Second, its walls have a rather strange shape.

The mountain is called Kolvir. It rises high behind us, and at its summit is a flight of three steps. You won't have time to see this, of course, but on a brightly moonlit night a city appears above the summit, and shimmering stairs connect with the steps. This is Tir-na Nog'th, the reflection of Amber in the sky.

The layout is pentagonal. The reason is simple. It is an architectual approximation of the crown of Amber. In fact, as you'll see later, it's very close indeed.

Oh, yes, those globes atop the corners? They're

magical. If you don't believe it, try besieging the place. Trust me: you'll never get through.

To the left, then. Eastwards, if you will.

First we pass through a thicket of blue spruce (A). Next to ponderosa pine, blue spruce makes up the most of Kolvir's tree life. Then Kolvir slopes gently upwards, and we are alongside the northeast wall. Over there are the ruins (B).

Near here is a trellised area (C), and the walkway through it leads to a series of formal gardens (D). They are very much like the gardens found in eighteenth-century Japan (in your Shadow), and Benedict, who tends them, is trying to expand them further. I find them rather too subdued, but Benedict's fascination with Oriental things is much stronger than any objection I might raise. Even so, there's no point actually going to look at them.

We're directly behind the castle now, in a park-like area of benches and walks (E). Many of my brothers and sisters come here to stroll, to think, even to become inspired. This is where Gerard tries to get his football games going. I use this place too, but usually only at night, and rarely by myself, though I do find it inspiring.

As you can see, beyond the walks is a small artificial lake (F). Past it, Benedict has begun another Japanese garden (G). Beside us, to the west, is a formal garden of the kind that was

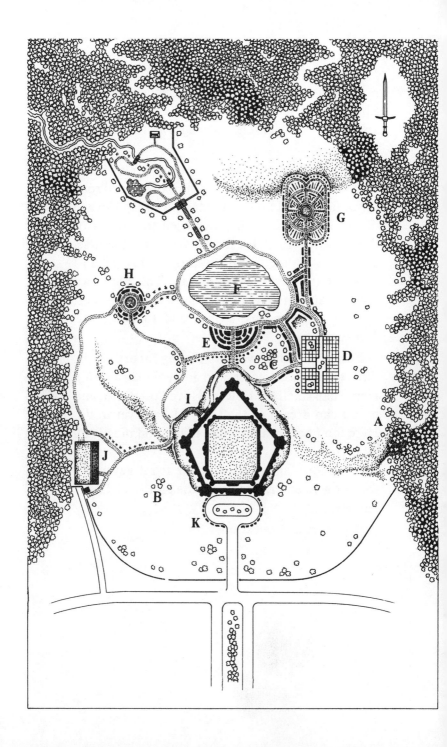

popular in eighteenth-century England in your Shadow (H). This one too I find a bit too proper and prim, but at least it has hedges and shrubs that I recognize.

Around the northwest corner now. Here, embedded in the ground, is a stair of natural rock formation (I). This is the stairway that Corwin climbed, when he and Bleys tried to overthrow their brother Eric. He didn't make it, of course, and he was blinded for his treason. Below us, on a grassy hill, are the stables (J). The only two noteworthy horses there right now are Benedict's, with its black and red stripes, and Julian's horse, Morgenstern.

Facing the southwest wall is my favorite area, filled with flowers, trees, and gorgeous shrubs (K). Here I can smell the flowers I loved on Earth, and here I can dream of the things I have yet to do. Here too I have wandered at night, and mostly all by myself.

And so we arrive back at the front gates. It's time now to enter, and to see the glories of Castle Amber.

Are there any questions?

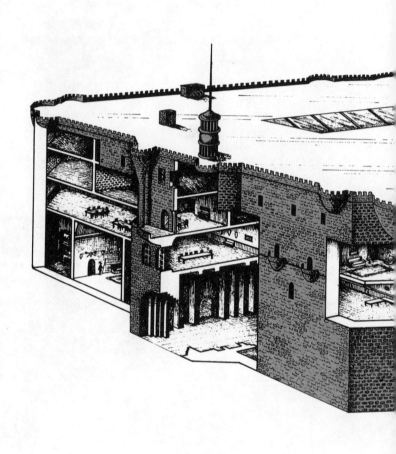

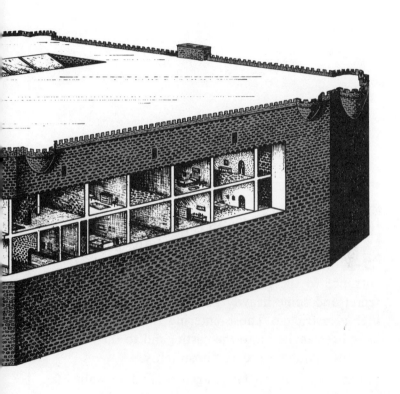

CASTLE
AMBER

THE MAIN HALL

he main hall, which is composed of false arches and columns that nearly hide the beamed ceiling, is of course the official entrance to the castle. There are others, some secret and some heavily guarded, but those are highly restricted. Those entering the main hall have been invited into the castle, and to them is extended Amber's greatest hospitality.

The floor here is a dark flagstone, and the walls are a white marble streaked with a deep bluish gray. Along the walls hang large, colorful tapestries, while ornate sconces cast a soft light into all corners. Doorways lead immediately to the left and the right, and a wide stairway leading upwards waits at the end of the hall.

The front doors themselves, which now stand open, close to form an arch. They are 15 feet high and 8 feet wide when together, and they are made of a dark, heavy wood that Oberon brought out of Shadow. Although not especially ornate, they are carved with several designs. The most important design is a stylized unicorn, half on each door. When they are closed, the Unicorn seals the castle.

Intriguing and addicting, the tapestries almost leap from the walls. Here are hunting scenes, pastoral scenes, and scenes of Amber's mythology. In one, Dworkin and the Unicorn compose *The Book of the Unicorn.* In another, the Pattern of Amber forms inside Kolvir. Another shows Oberon in chains in the dungeons of Chaos. The two largest are closest to the the stairway. The first shows Corwin and Bleys on the stair outside the castle, Shadow-warriors fallen around them and Eric standing defiantly in the doorway. The second depicts Corwin creating the Pattern, sparks about his grim face and exhaustion showing in his limbs.

Weapons and shields hang on the walls as well. Three notable ones are the halberd used by a guard to save Dworkin's life, the stiletto with which Paulette, Oberon's third wife, committed suicide, and a long, thin sword reported to be the sister-sword to Corwin's famous Grayswandir. Only Corwin could identify it for sure, but he is not here and no one can find him.

THE YELLOW ROOM AND FRONT SITTING ROOMS

Immediately inside the castle, two doors lead off the main hallway. On the right is the Yellow Room, so-called because it is constructed from a yellowish stone. The stone is close enough to Amber gold that the main throne was almost housed here. Even without the throne, however, this is still the room where the king grants audience, and from where he conducts the official business of the kingdom. As we'll see later, though, he does his actual work in his own chambers.

To the left are two sitting rooms. Outfitted in French provincial furniture, which Llewella claims she brought directly from Paris — a highly suspect claim, I might add. These rooms contain armchairs with rich upholstery, desks with quills and

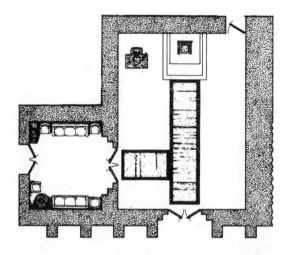

ink wells, fireplaces of the most exquisitely grained marble, and bookshelves filled with all sorts of reading material. Random thought it would be amusing to include some obscure authors working in the postmodernist phase of your Shadow, because he knew very well no visitor would understand them. Then he threw in some philosophical treatises which nobody can read, and some stuff about quantum mechanics that only Corwin could ever care about. Finally, he shifted into Shadow and retrieved two perfect, signed first editions of Corwin's rather self-indulgent chronicles. Strangely, a great many visitors appear to like them.

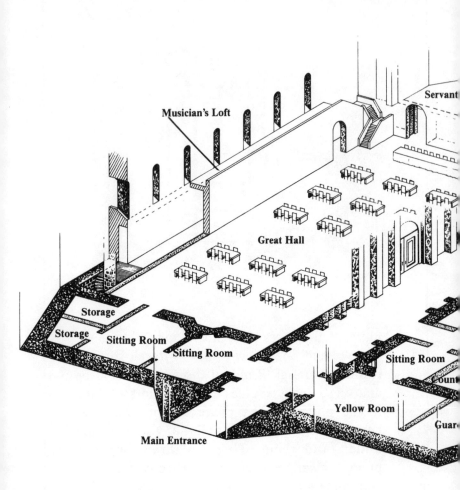

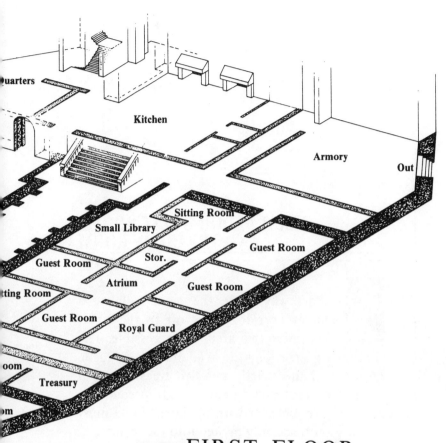

Quarters

Kitchen

Armory

Out

Sitting Room

Small Library

Guest Room

Guest Room

Stor.

Atrium

Guest Room

tting Room

Guest Room

Royal Guard

oom

Treasury

om

FIRST FLOOR
CASTLE
AMBER

FIRST FLOOR GUEST ROOMS
AND TREASURY ROOM

 short way down the main hallway, a smaller corridor leads off to the right. From here two areas are accessible. The first floor guest rooms are available for any castle guests, and the strictly guarded treasury room holds the kingdom's financial and bureaucratic heart. I rarely bother with the latter, but I must admit I am frequently invited into the former.

The guest rooms were primarily my own idea. I felt it would be both hospitable and useful to provide comfortable sitting areas, dens, and resting areas for guests on official business. All this was during the Interregnum, so permission was easy to come by. I simply told Eric what I wanted to do, went off into Shadow and got what I wanted. Then

26

had Amber's best carpenters fashion the rooms the way I envisioned them.

The result is the richly paneled, ornately decorated, thoroughly comfortable chambers you see before you. Some of the furniture comes right from Versailles, while other pieces have straggled in from such places as Vienna, Rome, Singapore, and even New Orleans. Of course, other Shadows contributed as well.

The guest rooms include two separate dining areas and four private resting areas. I have dined in the dining areas, and I have visited the resting areas. Infrequently, however, just to rest.

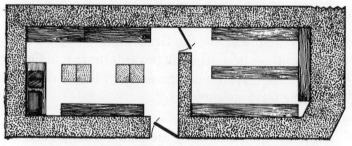

The treasury room has two guards on duty at all times, day, night, and Unicorn days. We are not allowed through these doors, so I will simply explain that the room contains the castle's vaults and all its important records. Only King Random is authorized to enter, and he cannot enter alone. A small anteroom immediately outside the vault room is for the guards.

THE KITCHEN
AND THE ARMORY

urther along the main hallway, a double door to the left leads into the Great Hall. Before seeing the Great Hall, though, we will continue down the hall towards the rear of the castle. Here are found the armory, the kitchen, and the servants' quarters.

For obvious reasons, we will not enter the servants' quarters. They are small, clean, single bedrooms, and there is a common table for dining. The only interesting feature about these rooms is a stairway that leads into the guest apartments on the second floor. Both Corwin and Merlin have used this stairway to steal into the kitchen and gorge themselves on food.

The armory is stocked with various armor and weaponry. Hanging along the wall, and stuffed into trunks and cabinets, are many historic mementos: Oberon's first set of ring-mail, still in excellent shape; the sword Corwin wore at Waterloo; Benedict's Japanese armor and swords, and the falchion Caine carried in the Spanish Main. Julian, too, has mementoes here: the full plate he bore in the Crusades, dented during the relief of Jerusalem; and the saber he carried at Balaclava. Unlike the rest of the Light Brigade, he was able to trump out.

Random has suggested that these mementoes be displayed throughout the castle, but all the princes have objected. Since the armorers keep them in excellent repair, they argue, why not leave them in the armory? Who knows when they might become useful again?

A large door from the armory leads out towards the outer wall.

The kitchen is enormous. The huge fireplace on the rear wall controls the heat for the several ovens and spits that project from it. Shelves line the walls, and they are filled with pots, pans, utensils, and other cooking paraphernalia. A long table on the west wall is used for food preparation, and the large walk-in icebox in the northeast corner keeps the meat and fruit fresh. The largest of the spits is used to roast the bigger animals. Shortly, the cooks have promised me, the smell of roasting beef will fill this part of the castle.

29

THE GREAT HALL

he most sacred room in Castle Amber, the Great Hall bears much of the kingdom's history. It was here that Oberon wed each of his wives, and it was here that Random brought Vialle, for a feast in her honor, after she returned with him from Rebma as his wife. Here Dworkin placed the newly crafted crown of Amber on the head of Oberon, and here Oberon laid the body of Paulette in state for ten agonizing days. Others have lain in state here as well: Eric, Caine, Dierdre, and Corwin.

The problem with Corwin, though, was that he wasn't really dead. We thought he was, so we fashioned a coffin and a tomb for him and went through the ritual of laying him in state. When he showed up, several years later, that earlier ceremony became considerably less important.

30

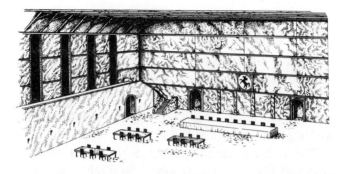

This is the room where the guards led Corwin, during the ceremony in which Eric was crowned king. At the front of this room, Corwin took the crown and placed it on his own head, in an act that threw real doubt on Eric's claim to the throne. Later, in a sadder but stabler time, Random was crowned King by all the royal family, and at the same occasion we embraced Vialle as our Queen.

I met a traveller from an antique land that night. His legs were strong, and they were not trunkless.

The Great Hall measures approximately 50 feet wide and 90 feet long. Its beamed and plastered ceiling is almost 40 feet above the ground. On the south wall, doorways lead into the sitting rooms, while on the north wall two doors lead to the corridor near the kitchen. A bar stands in the northeast corner, and Random and Corwin have ensured its stock is generous and excellent. Even

31

from here, I can taste the fullness of the nineteenth-century French grape.

A long table stretches along that north wall. During feasts, this is of course the head table. Well-spaced on the floor is a host of smaller tables. At a feast the guests will fill many; others will bear crafts, goods, and artworks from the city.

The lighting in the Great Hall seems to be reflected through a soft jewel. Sunlight streams through the bevelled windows (which begin over 25 feet up the wall) down towards the floor. The effect is almost prismatic, and the Hall takes on a beautiful, hypnotic shimmer. Because of this shimmer, the deep green vein in the white marble walls seems to slither its way from the ceiling to the floor. Under a bright moon, the vein actually dominates. The Great Hall at night is eerie.

Against the center of the north wall stands a statue of the Unicorn. Carved from black and white marble, its stance is the mirror image of the Unicorn design on the front doors. Its horn points towards the windows on the western wall, and it seems to beckon the sunlight. On nonfestive occasions, the Unicorn is behind a set of rich, green curtains.

Lower on the west wall are the elaborate shields of the Golden Circle kingdoms. The shield of Gaiga bears a single tree, while Kashfa's shows a tall mountain with three stars off to its left side. On

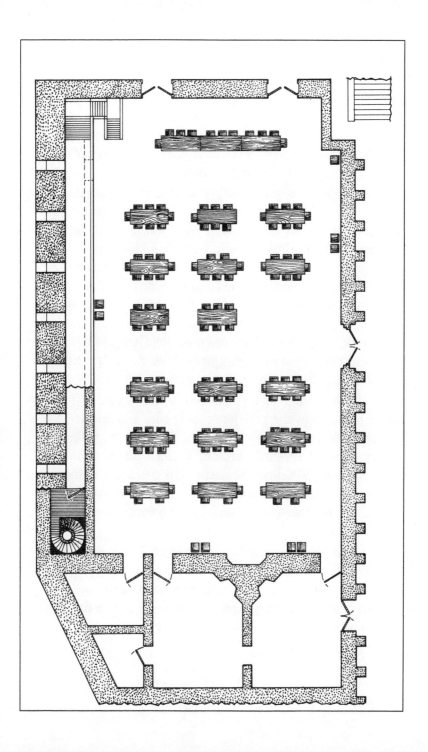

Begma's shield a sword points downwards, and on Eregnor's a single tower rises into a blue sky. The shields confirm the Golden Circle treaty. In the corresponding Halls of those kingdoms, Amber's Unicorn graces a shield of its own.

Behind the west wall, the throne is securely stored. It is brought out only for special occasions, and Random has used it only once — at his coronation. Carved from a single slab of golden amber, the throne is embellished with several important symbols. The Unicorn is one, of course, but an abstraction of the Pattern is the most impressive. A mysterious face is carved on the back of the throne. No one knows who it represents, but the consensus suggests Dworkin. In the moonlight, the eyes seem to move.

The storage space is actually a hallway. Off-limits to anyone but the royal family and selected guards, the hallway leads to a set of spiral stairs that wind upwards around a thick column and downwards below the castle. Up the stairs is the door to the musician's gallery, 20 feet above the floor of the Great Hall. Downwards are the dungeons.

The column that the stairs circle is deceptive. While it appears solid, in fact it houses a steep, narrow stairway. This is the stairway Corwin used to reach the library, and all of us have at one time climbed it. Why it exists at all, nobody knows.

DUNGEONS

CASTLE AMBER

THE STAIRWAY INTO KOLVIR

he spiral stairway leads down, from the corridor behind the Great Hall. The descent is long, very long in fact, and the route back up is exhausting beyond belief. Fortunately for us, however, Random knows we're here. He will have his son Martin waiting for us above. One by one, I will trump us all out.

Eons ago, this stair was built around a great central shaft into Kolvir's heart. Who constructed it and how it was done remains a complete and total mystery. Oberon might have known, but if he told one of us that person has never spoken up. The likeliest answer is that the stair follows a natural set of linked caves, and that all the builder had to do was to knock out the walls that separated the caves from one another.

To your own Shadow, the stairway leading down is one of the most terrifying possible encounters. Apart from horror movies, which use it widely, it was the inspiration for many myths of the underworld, and even the focal point of some of your psychologies. The underground is dark, and the air is not fresh.

For us, though, this stairway is two things. First and least attractive, it leads to the dungeons below the castle. All castles have dungeons, although the varieties are many, and like them we must have some place to lock away prisoners and treachers. But there's a  positive side to the spiral stair as well. For beyond the dungeons, in a special room behind a locked door, the Pattern of Amber is etched into the floor. It glows, and it summons us, and it controls the fate of all Shadow.

King Random has given permission for you to see it. But before we go there, we must look upon the dungeons. Some of the sights you will not like. I can only guarantee you that all are necessary, for the safety of Amber, and thus for your Shadow as well.

GUARDS' STATIONS
AND THE DUNGEONS

f course, dungeons need guards. On occasion, a prisoner escapes. On others, one finds his way down here. In either case, the guard locks him up and reports him to the king. The guard has other duties as well. He is in charge of keeping the tunnels clean. He also feeds the prisoners. They don't get much, but they get enough to keep them alive. Not that all of them want to stay that way.

At the guards' station, keys hang on several hooks in the wall. These are the keys to the dungeon cells. Beside them hang lanterns, necessary to find one's way through the tunnels. The tunnels themselves are easy to traverse, but to the inexperienced they are something of a maze.

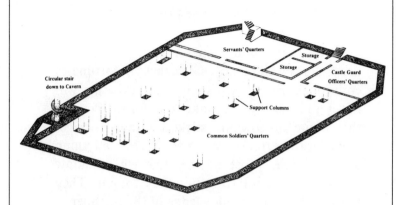

Off the main tunnel, many other tunnels lead. Exactly how many isn't known, because not all have been explored. In fact, Amber has lost some escaped prisoners, when they have managed to avoid the guard and slip down an unpatrolled tunnel. But as far as is known, these tunnels lead nowhere.

The first tunnel holds the political prisoners. Each cell is lined with straw, which the guard replaces weekly. These prisoners are fed daily, and every third day they are interrogated. If they are important enough, one of the royal family performs the interrogation. At one time or another, each of the Golden Circle kingdoms has had a representative in these cells. The most recent was a prince of Gaiga, who was sentenced for espionage against Amber. After a six-month stay, he broke and explained all. Oberon sent for Gaiga's king, and a treaty was worked out. The prince was released. He has never returned.

Down the second tunnel are the cells for the prisoners of war. In most cases, these unfortunates come out of Shadow. Also in most cases, they will never go back. Amber makes attempts to contact their home Shadows and strike a suitable arrangement for their return, but in few cases is anything accomplished. Most of the time, the Shadow doesn't even want to admit they fought. They frequently claim no knowledge of the prisoner.

The third tunnel is given over to Amber's own criminals. Murderers' Row, it is called, because most of the criminals have done just that. Grand thieves are put here as well, as are those who desecrate a statue of the Unicorn. One court jester was brought here after urinating on Oberon's throne. He was released after seventeen years. As jester, he was finished.

The fourth tunnel holds those convicted of treason. Throughout the ages it has imprisoned many important and famous Amberites, but none more famous than Prince Corwin. For the only time in Amber's history, a member of the royal family was held in the dungeons. The idea was Eric's, and it was not popular.

A brassbound door opens into Corwin's cell. Barely large enough to lie straight in, the cell

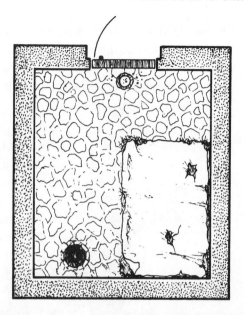

has been left exactly as it was when Corwin escaped. Some dirty straw lies scattered about, but most of it has been gathered into a pile now blackened by fire. A hole in the far corner served as a latrine. On the inside of the door, gouges indicate where Corwin had carved at the door with the sharpened handle of his spoon.

On the far wall is carved a sketch. According to Corwin, Dworkin drew it, an unbelievably fine outline of the lighthouse of Cabra. If stared at too long, it might still transport the viewer to the lighthouse. The wall to its right bears another sketch. This one is a view of a den, perhaps a

41

library. Bookshelves line the walls, a desk stands in the foreground, and a large globe rests on the floor beside it. On the desk rests a small human skull, while on the wall behind a tall candlestick rises. The flame on the candle is flickering.

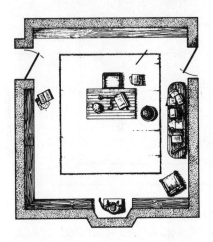

As you stare, the sketch comes alive. Closer examination now reveals bookshelves on all four walls and no windows on any. There are two doors at the far end of the room, one to the right and the other to the left. Beside the left door, a long, low table is covered with books and papers. On the bookshelves and in recesses in the walls are bizarre curios — bones, stones, pottery, inscribed tablets, lenses, wands, and various obscure instruments. A huge Ardebil rug covers the floor.

This is Dworkin's chamber. At least, so the rumors say. Corwin in his narrative describes a visit to that chamber, and he has more to say about what lies within.

Through the left door, he says, is a small, windowless living space. The room's stone walls form an arch. A fireplace stands on the left wall, and in the far wall a wide, armored door guards what Corwin claims is the entrance to the primal Pattern.

We must turn from the sketch now, before it draws us in. If we enter the chamber of Dworkin, we shall not likely return.

THE DUNGEONS AND
THE PATTERN OF AMBER

The fifth tunnel houses the insane. In your Shadow, they would be treated more kindly. Here, they are merely kept alive. One of the insane is fascinating. He claims to be an author, and he insists that Amber is his subject. So mad is he that he says he — and not Corwin —composed the tale of Corwin's fight against the black road and the Courts of Chaos. But the best part is his demand to see Prince Corwin. The prince, he says, knows him by name. We've had many insanes, but he is the most amusing. Gerard thinks we should release him, but Random is unsure. If Corwin returns, we will certainly ask his advice.

The sixth tunnel is the home of loathsome creatures from Shadow. They are terrifying, and we will not visit them. Some have the power of absolute hypnosis. They are fed only by the blind.

The seventh tunnel leads to the Pattern of Amber. A great, dark, metal-bound door blocks its opening, but all Amberian royals have a key. When it opens, all lamps can be extinguished. The glow is from the Pattern itself. When eyes adjust, they see it in the center of the room. It appears as a shining, shimmering mass of curved lines, inscribed into the stone floor, lines that fool the eye as it tries to trace them. To a Amberian non-royal the lines are almost blinding; to anyone not from Amber they are hypnotic as well. This room is not for casual visitors.

The Pattern begins in the far corner. From there, the walker places one foot down carefully after the other, until after expending great energy the Pattern's center comes into sight. Upon reaching the center, the walker, by an act of will, can go to any desired location. Only those whose veins bear the blood of Amber may walk the Pattern and live.

We return now, to the main hallway. I have taken a trump from my pocket. Concentrating on it, I see the face of Martin, complete with Mohawk haircut. Now, his hand has appeared. One by one, you will touch his hand. For a brief second you will feel disoriented, but when everything settles down you will find yourself at the bottom of the stairway that leads up to the second floor. When we are all gathered there, I will show you more of the castle.

CASTLE AMBER

p these stairs is the castle's second and third floors. Much of the fourth floor is not being used right now, with some rooms under development and others simply awaiting future needs. The fourth floor is the most recent addition to the castle; Oberon constructed it when it became obvious he was going to sire a number of offspring.

All but two of the royal family have their apartments on the second floor. The exceptions are Random, who occupies the king's apartments, and mine. I had a third floor apartment specially designed. Many of my siblings protested, but things were so chaotic during the Interregnum I got it done anyway. I spend a fair bit of time in the castle, and the second floor apartments were simply too cramped.

There are two things to keep in mind while visiting the various apartments. First, the royal family spends very little time in the castle, so rooms may not be neat. Second, each is decorated according to personal taste, so there is no sense of continuity in style or color. Normally, we do not venture into each others' rooms. But for the sake of this visit Random contacted each of the royals by their trumps, and all agreed to let us in. A few, though, trumped home long enough to tidy up and to hide things.

47

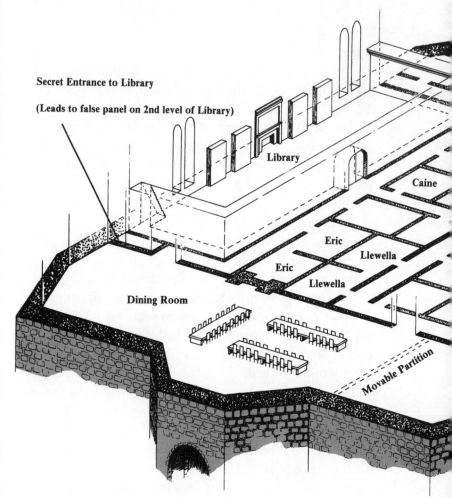

Secret Entrance to Library

(Leads to false panel on 2nd level of Library)

Library

Caine

Eric

Llewella

Eric

Llewella

Dining Room

Movable Partition

Note: Unmarked Rooms are:
1. Guest Rooms
2. Storage
3. Sitting Rooms

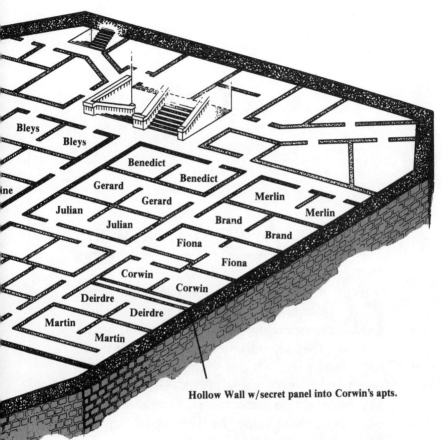

Bleys

Bleys

Benedict

Benedict

Gerard

ine

Gerard

Julian

Julian

Merlin

Merlin

Brand

Brand

Fiona

Fiona

Corwin

Corwin

Deirdre

Deirdre

Martin

Martin

Hollow Wall w/secret panel into Corwin's apts.

SECOND FLOOR
CASTLE
AMBER

GUEST APARTMENTS

t the top of the stairs are the guest apartments, above the armory, kitchen, and servants' quarters. As their name suggests, they are occupied only when the castle has visitors on official business. During the negotiations with each of the Golden Circle kingdoms, the apartments were filled at all times. Since then, though, they have remained empty or underused much of the time.

Like the guest sitting rooms on the first floor, these apartments have sitting areas, dining areas, and a small library. They also have bedrooms, however, and the beds here are among the best in the castle. That was Random's influence, who believes in the guests' comfort much more than Oberon ever did. The satin sheets were my idea.

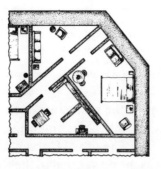

A small stairway from the servants' quarters leads upwards into the guest apartments. The castle's servants are at the beck and call of the guests, and only rarely has a guest abused this privilege. In one instance, a prince from Eregnor awoke in the middle of the night and called for a meal. Two servants leaped from their beds and scrambled to get to him, but they weren't fast enough. By the time they managed to reach his apartments, he was out in the corridor, wielding a sword, denouncing Amber at the top of his lungs. The noise was so great it awoke Oberon, who raced downstairs in his nightshirt with a saber in his hand. Soon we all heard the sound of steel on steel; in less than a minute all of us were in the corridor in our nightclothes. We separated the two, then looked at each other and laughed. Oberon laughed, too, but he didn't forget. One of Eregnor's key demands disappeared from the treaty that very night.

The prince got his meal, though.

51

"Yes. I am a sorcerer. I am Merlin, son of Corwin of Amber and Dara of the Courts of Chaos, known to local friends and acquaintances as Merle Corey: bright, charming, witty, athletic . . . . Go read Castiglione and Lord Byron for particulars, as I'm modest, aloof and reticent, as well."

Merlin is one of the new generation of royal descendants. But he's somewhat unusual in his origins. The son of Corwin of Amber and Dara of Chaos, he was raised in the Courts of Chaos, where he became an initiate of the Logrus, which is Chaos's unformed version of the Pattern. He became interested in Amber and in Shadow after his father told him the story found in the Chronicles of Amber. Since that time, he has come to the castle quite frequently.

His room reflects his esoteric tastes. A large, colorful Oriental rug covers most of the sitting room floor. Depicting a hunting scene in a forest, its line of trees almost overwhelms the entire room. To counter its dominance, he has chosen only a simple sofa with two chairs as furniture for that room.

The bedroom is neat, which suggests he hasn't been here recently. Beside the armoire are sprawled his characteristic jogging shoes, and these suggest all the time he spent in your Shadow's California. Once he brought to the castle a machine he called a laptop portable computer, but he soon found it would not work. Another time he mentioned hang-gliding off Kolvir's summit.

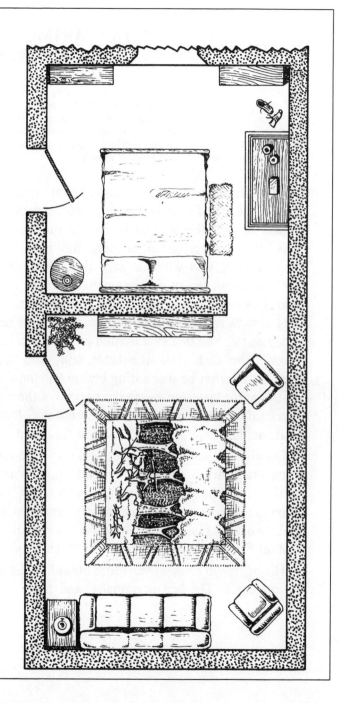

BRAND'S APARTMENTS

"Then there was a figure both like Bleys and myself. My features, though smaller, my eyes, Bleys's hair, beardless. He wore a riding suit of green and sat atop a white horse, heading toward the dexter side of the card. There was a quality of both strength and weakness, questing and abandonment about him. I both approved and disapproved, liked and was repelled by, this one. His name was Brand, I knew. As soon as I laid eyes upon him, I knew." (from Corwin's Chronicles)

clectic and tasteless, Brand's room reflects the man's volatile temperament. It reflects as well the interest he had in magic. On Random's orders the apartment has been left exactly as it was when Brand died. We know nothing about the rug in the sitting room, except that it came from an unspecified Shadow. Brand was always reticent about explaining any of his possessions, and he never invited anyone into his room. The dishes on the table still hold the remains of what he was eating before leaving the castle for the last time, but the papers show that he was studying the history and the mythology of the Pattern. This would fit well with his final end.

On his desk are more papers, and these too are connected with a study of the Pattern. A black leather easy chair sits in a corner, with a still-full glass of red wine on the round table beside it. At its feet, two books lie closed. These are books from a distant Shadow, and they speak of black magic.

His bedroom reveals even more of his interest in black magic. The bed is unmade, and more unwashed glasses rest on the night table. On the desk in the corner, several instruments of magic await their user. One is some kind of voodoo doll. Another is a mysterious skeleton. Jars and vials of only partly identified substances are pushed to the back.

From the northwest corner of the bedroom, two chains extend from the wall. Ashes are scattered nearby. It has never been ascertained what these chains were used for, but it is fairly certain that Brand had begun to practice human sacrifice. At the very least, he was a torturer.

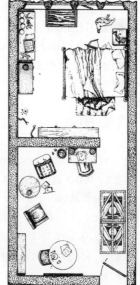

The book on the work-desk, is a copy of *The Book of the Unicorn*, Dworkin's masterpiece. A search through the drawers suggests that Brand, when he died, was attempting to create a trump of the book, and that he would shortly try to trump himself back to the book's creation. We have had many debates about the possibility of doing this, but everything has proven inconclusive. Many of Brand's ideas remain unexamined, and most of us feel they should stay that way.

"Then there was Fiona, with hair like Bleys or Brand, my eyes, and a complexion like mother of pearl. I hated her the second I turned over the card." (from Corwin's Chronicles)

iona has decorated her apartments in what Shadow Earth would call contemporary Scandinavian. I detest all modern Earth styles, but I find her decor fascinating. Every time I enter her room I find something new and interesting to explore. But please don't tell her this.

The most notable feature is the hand-stitched ryaa rug that covers over half her sitting room. This rug, whose resiliency seems to absorb the feet of any who step on it, is directly from the Swiss town of Rya. Fiona claims it is from the best designer of ryaa rugs, and that he made it especially for her.

The sleek sculpture in the corner is by an unknown artist. But knowing Fiona's capabilities, the sculptor is probably among the best artists of the century. The desk (Scandinavian again) shows a book of contemporary European short fiction, translated into English under the title "Aberrational Fictions/Operational Functions." Apparently, she actually reads this stuff.

The bedroom is noteworthy primarily because of its neatness. The Scandinavian designs emphasize simplicity and sparseness, which Fiona

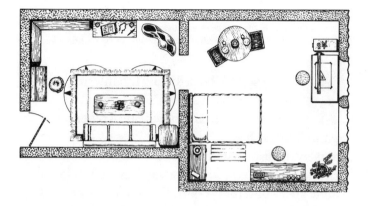

turns to very good advantage. Even her plants are few and beautifully kept, and her drafting table displays the kind of precise, measured art she finds worthwhile. Her table sports the finest British china, and even her window-sills contain but two long, sleek statuettes.

The south wall abuts Corwin's bedroom wall. During Corwin's absence, Fiona often reported sounds of a sobbing woman from within his apartments. When Corwin returned, he confirmed her stories. According to him, his apartments had always been haunted, apparently by Oberon's first wife. Oberon would say nothing about her, though, and her spirit has not yet managed to speak. Since Corwin's recent disappearance, the ghost has not returned.

"Green eyes, black hair, dressed in black and silver, yes. I had on a cloak and it was slightly furled as by a wind. I had on black boots, like Eric's, and I too wore a blade, only mine was heavier, though not quite as long as his. I had my gloves on and they were silver and scaled. The clasp at my neck was cast in the form of a silver rose." (from Corwin's Chronicles)

ong deserted, both during the Interregnum and currently, Corwin's apartments have been tidied and cleaned as Amber once again awaits his return. As always, they are sparsely furnished, with utility the major decorative criterion. An antique roll-away desk contains a single sheet of paper. On it, Corwin has scrawled roughly 20 obscure symbols, none of which any of the royal family recognizes. Merlin suspects that Corwin learned this code during his conversation with Dworkin, but Vialle intuits that the code is a communication system used in the Courts of Chaos. Merlin, who was born in Chaos, disagrees.

A reading chair sits in the center of the sitting room. Along the west wall is a matching loveseat. Two small bookshelves stand on the other two walls, along with a shelf for other displays.

In addition to several books taken from Shadow, the bookshelves contain a wealth of books from the Renaissance of Shadow Earth. Among these is a complete set of Shakespearean folios and quartos, one of which proves conclusively that the Bard had nothing to do with the history play Henry VIII. A folio of *Hamlet, Prince*

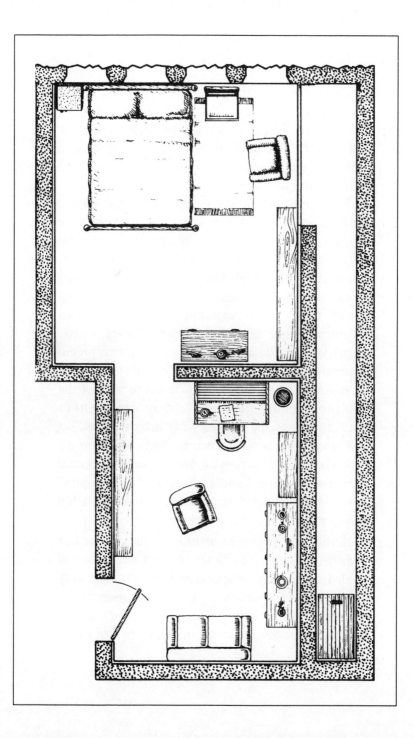

of Denmark bears the playwright's initials, as well as a friendly greeting addressed to Corwin. Also on this shelf are editions and manuscripts of Castiglione's *The Courtier*, Machiavelli's *The Prince*, and several editions of Rabelais and Cervantes.

Later publications show other areas of Corwin's interest. *Defoe's Journal of the Plague Year* appears well-used, perhaps because Corwin himself was infected and lived during that plague. Several books deal with the subject of song composition, and there are collections of song lyrics from the Renaissance to the twentieth century. Other books detail art history, music history, and the most significant philosophical and scientific treatises. A new interest seems to be in quantum mechanics. On the north wall of the bedroom hangs Oberon's riding crop. Other mementoes of the former King are displayed on the bookcase, several from the days of Oberon's disquise as Ganelon. Also on that shelf is a small metal spoon, its handle sharpened to a jagged point. Corwin never revealed why he kept such a grisly memento of his imprisonment.

A safe stands in the northeast corner. None but Corwin know the combination, so it has remained sealed during his disappearance. Behind the easy chair on the south wall is an entrance to an extremely narrow corridor. At the end of that corridor, a door in the floor opens to a narrow

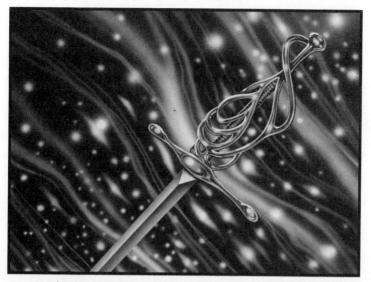

stairway leading up to the third floor, and perhaps beyond to the unused fourth. What Corwin used it for, or whether he used it at all, is unknown to all but himself.

Two guitars rest against the wall beside the chair. The first is of twentieth century manufacture, a gift to Corwin from Segovia. The second, Corwin's prize possession, is the only Stradivarius guitar ever built. Fiona remembers hearing, through the wall that joined their rooms, the sounds of Corwin strumming this beautiful instrument: the bass was deep and shimmering, while the high frets were sweet, sad, and hypnotic. She often felt that Corwin had more passion than any were willing to credit.

DEIRDRE'S APARTMENTS

"And then there was a black-haired girl with the same blue eyes, and her hair hung long and she was dressed all in black, with a girdle of silver about her waist. My eyes filled with tears, why I don't know. Her name was Deirdre." (from Corwin's Chronicles)

ike the apartments of Eric, Brand, and Caine, Deirdre's has been preserved as it was prior to her death. Deirdre was dear to many of the royals, and most of them dislike even thinking about the fact of her death. They do not speak of her, as if they had an unspoken agreement not to.

Deirdre updated her decor regularly. At the time of her death, she had just redecorated in an elegant, modern Manhattan-style. The chairs are geniune Frank Lloyd Wright designs, and the floor and furniture stylings would be completely at home in the famous Dakotas apartment complex. Typical for her, she was the first to comfort the bereaved Yoko Ono.

Her bedroom is equally tasteful, equally modern, and equally expensive. But the most notable item in the room, and also the saddest, is the dress that lies atop the bed. Dark green silk, she had intended to wear it to a New York City welcome of the Prince and Princess of Wales. As beautiful as she was, she would have completely overshadowed the princess. She would never have shown it, but she would have smiled inside when that happened.

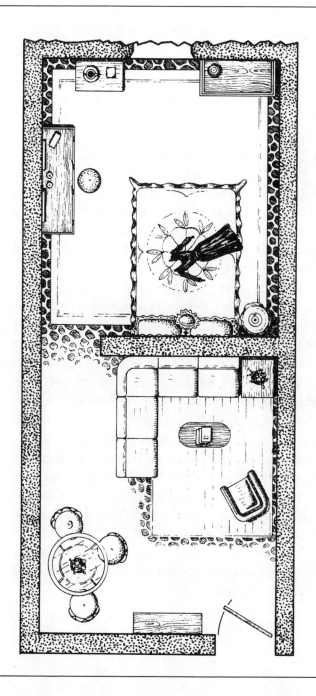

"I sat to Random's left, Martin to his right. I hadn't seen Martin in a long while and was curious what he'd been about . . . . Although he resembled Random, Martin looked a little less sneaky, and he was taller. Still, he was not a really big guy." (from Merlin's Chronicles)

The son of Random and Morganthe of Rebma, Martin is the natural heir to the throne of Amber. Of course, if Random died right now and Martin made his claim, every Amber royal would step in and stop him. But technically he's the one on whom the future of Amber rests.

When he first started coming to Amber, he was a typical youth — typical for an Amberite, that is. He was tall and thin, gangly and shy. He was dressed in subdued, respectable clothes, and he spoke carefully and only when asked to. But something has happened to him recently. He seems to have developed a rebellious streak.

For one thing, he now sports a Mohawk haircut. True, with his Amber-Rebma blood and skin hue he could pass for a Native Indian, but he looks ridiculous. Even his father rolls his eyes whenever Martin enters the dining room. Coupled with his torn blue jeans and fringed jacket, the Mohawk makes him dated even on Shadow Earth. Here, of course, one usually dresses formally. Several centuries behind the times, but formally nevertheless.

Like his father, Martin is a drummer. But where Random loves jazz, Martin insists on rock. The door to his apartments opens to reveal a series of posters on the far wall, each showing a rock star or group of Shadow Earth of the 1980s. He claims his musical favorites are serious and oriented towards the non-commercial, but to me they all simply look strange.

Who could listen, for instance, to the Dead Delivery Boys? Or to the Vomiteers? Or this group, Skeletal Boogie? He has even started his own group, and he says the Hellriders have just signed a recording contract. Their first album will be called "Forever Amber."

Martin has part of his record collection stored here. He tried to bring a portable phonograph, but of course it wouldn't work. What he ended up with, finally, was a late-model gramophone, which he acquired by Shadow-shifting to 1950s San Francisco. Since Deirdre's room is empty, he turns it up to full volume and blasts his mind away. Only his father ever listens to music with him. To avoid problems, Martin also brought with him some early Buddy Rich, Random's favorite artist.

THE UNUSED GUEST APARTMENTS AND DINING ROOM

n addition to the guest apartments at the north end of this floor, several apartments have been set aside for future use, or should the castle have a multitude of unexpected guests descend upon it. Since guests to Castle Amber must be invited, the only way this could happen is for an invited party to bring with them, unannounced, a retinue the castle does not want.

It has happened only once. The occasion was the drafting of the peace treaty and the trading treaty with Kashfa. The King of Kashfa, an ostentatious man, was to come to Amber with only his wife, his two sons, and his three daughters. The north-end guest apartments had just enough room for the family, but Oberon prepared the unused guest apartments in case the Kashfans felt cramped. As it turns out, this was a good thing.

When the Kashfans came through the door, Oberon's eyes almost leaped from his head. Behind the Kashfan royal family stood a retinue of almost 46 people: servants, ladies in waiting, grooms, and the like. Oberon took one look, then turned and marched away. He summoned all the castle's servants and gave them orders to prepare the guest apartments to accommodate them all. They managed, and the week went by relatively uneventfully.

The result, though, was a set of small bedrooms rather than comfortable apartments. They remain this way still, and no one knows if they will ever be used again. With the Golden Circle kingdoms and Amber currently in a time of excellent peace, visiting parties from the kingdoms tend to be small. Rarely do we see one of their royal families.

The Great Hall is used for formal and state dining occasions. Indeed, it is often called the large marble dining room. But the royal family almost never eats there. Instead, they have meals sent to their rooms, or, less frequently, they dine together in the second floor dining room. Under Random's rule, these communal dinners have become increasingly common.

The second floor hallways leads directly to the dining room. A double doorway leads inside. Immediately across the room, along the outside wall, a series of windows looks out over the city. Three of the windows have window-seats, where the royal family will often sit, after the meal, and discuss Amber, politics, or perhaps each other.

The dining room occupies the entire front of the castle, but it is divided into two sections. The western section, larger than the other, is the dining room proper. The eastern portion is used by the cooks and the servants for the preparation of the meals. Since the main kitchen is a floor down and the length of the castle away, smaller ovens are needed to warm the food when it arrives, and to keep warm the various courses as the diners await them. The preparation room also holds the china, the cutlery, and the drinking cups and glasses.

The dining tables are long, each seating eight people comfortably. Like the chairs, they are constructed from strong, excellent wood, much like oak except a deeper and richer natural hue. Covering the tables during the meal are white tablecloths fringed with gold embroidery. Each was a gift from a Golden Circle kingdom. All of those kingdoms revere the cloth arts much more than Amber itself does.

In the far western corner is a small raised stage. At every meal, hired musicians play soft music for the royal family as they eat. For most, the music's merit is that it allows for private conversation with a neighboring royal. Without the music, the talk would be overheard.

In many ways, in fact, the conversations are the basis of the meal. It is far from unusual for diners to switch seats in mid-meal, to sit beside the person they wish to talk to. Most dinner-table conversations are conducted in low voices, even though few are actually secretive. The low voices have become an Amberite habit, the result of the years of internal dissension during the Interregnum. At that time, everyone suspected everyone else.

Meals themselves are eclectic affairs. All of the royals have their preferred cuisine, and some have conducted one of the castle cooks into Shadow to teach him how to prepare it. Benedict, for instance, has taken his favorite cook to nineteenth-century Japan on several occasions, and a full Japanese feast is a monthly event in the castle. Deirdre went through a vegetarian phase, and even though she dropped the custom before her death, the others have requested the vegetarian dinners be continued. Other dinners range from all parts of Shadow Earth, and even Begman and Eregnorian meals have begun to make an appearance. On state occasions, however, the venerable roast pig and roast cow make their succulent appearance.

It need hardly be mentioned that the wine list is enormous.

LLEWELLA'S APARTMENTS

"Next was Llewella, whose hair matched her jade-colored eyes, dressed in shimmering gray and green with a lavender belt, and looking moist and sad. For some reason, I knew she was not like the rest of us. But she, too, was my sister." (from Corwin's Chronicles)

lewella's apartments hold one of the castle's only decorative motifs. Her fascination is with Venus, the Graeco-Roman goddess of love, whom she claims to have met during her first Shadow-shift. As a result of this near-obsession, her rooms bear a beautiful seashell motif. Practically everything in the room supports this motif.

The loveseat and matching chairs are shaped and colored like seashells, whle the sitting room carpet is fringed to resemble seashells. A collection of shells from various Shadows is displayed on the sitting room bookcase, while atop the table sits a large, beautiful shell from what Llewella describes as "an ocean under Neptune's direct rule." Only the table itself is not shell-shaped, but its surface is a blue glass that resembles clear sea water.

In the bedroom, a shell-shaped desk sits against one wall, while a conch-shell vanity stands along another. The bedclothes are sea-colored, and the rug reflects the light in a way that seems to move like the gentle waves of calm seas. On the wall are several paintings that bear the Venus motif.

I've spent a few nights in this room. By the morning, I find myself seasick. The decor is overwhelming.

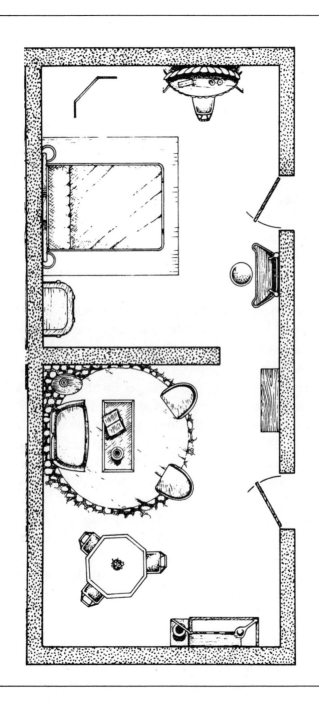

CAINE'S APARTMENTS

"Then came the swarthy, dark-eyed countenance of Caine, dressed all in satin that was black and green, wearing a dark three-cornered hat set at a rakish angle, a green plume of feathers trailing down the back. He was standing in profile, one arm akimbo, and the toes of his boots curled upwards, and he wore an emerald-studded dagger at his belt. There was ambivalence in my heart." (from Corwin's Chronicles)

lthough not as completely motif-oriented as Llewella's rooms, Caine's apartments clearly demonstrate his great interest in the navy and all military matters. After Caine's funeral, Random entered the apartments and decided to leave everything exactly as it had been. Unlike Brand, Caine was tidy, so there was little to straighten up even had Random wanted.

A large, fringed rug occupies the northwest side of the sitting room. On it, in the corner, a small bench displays naval artifacts from Caine's many journeys. In the middle of the rug stands a large table of thick oak. Maps, scattered atop it, show island areas of Shadow Earth, the Amber seas, and oceans of other Shadows. A telescope rests on a tripod in the southeast corner of the room. Caine's love was the sailing ship, and it was often suspected that he spent his early Shadow-shifting days as a privateer or in the English navy.

The bedroom maintains the nautical motif. Models of ships are displayed on two dressers, while a wooden ship's wheel hangs above the bed. Caine insisted that the wheel was from the *Pinta*, but nobody bothered to verify it. An antique

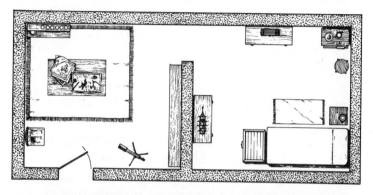

trunk stands at the foot of a bunklike single bed — he's the only royal who opted for a single bed — and inside it are maps, charts, weather calculations, and a host of other nautical paraphernalia. The walls display military maps of Caine's greatest battles. Front and center is the defense of Amber against the navies of Bleys and Corwin. Underneath it is a military map of the Battle of Trafalgar.

Caine was mysterious, but he was also highly romantic. Swarthy and dark-eyed, he wore his black and green satin wholly to his advantage, and I have no doubt he obsessed women wherever he traveled. I admired him for his exploits, and I longed for a man with half his romanticism. He is our most recent loss, and he is sorely missed.

JULIAN'S APARTMENTS

"Next, there was the passive countenance of Julian, dark hair hanging long, blue eyes containing neither passion nor compassion. He was dressed completely in scaled white armor, not silver or metallic-colored, but looking as if it had been enameled. I knew, though, that it was terribly tough and shock-resistant, despite its decorative and festive appearance. He was the man I had beaten at his favorite game, for which he had thrown a glass of wine at me. I knew him and I hated him."(from Corwin's Chronicles)

cross the hallway from Caine's rooms, Julian's rooms open to reveal a completely different lifestyle. Sparsely decorated, and every bit as attractive as a second-class hotel. The room shows that Julian is considerably less than neat and tidy, that he is interested in hunting big game, and that he wants nothing to tarnish his tough, masculine image.

In the corner behind the door, unopened boxes are stacked and scattered. A large, locked chest, under them, its contents are only to be speculated about. Two simple armchairs flank a small bookcase, which contains small paintings of hunting scenes. The only noteworthy feature in the sitting room is a sabre-tooth tiger-skin rug, sprawled on the floor. It is soft, warm, beautiful, and suits Julian perfectly.

The bedroom is equally sparse, with two dressers, a small chair, and an uncluttered desk. The bookcase-style headboard shows artifacts collected from Arden Forest, as well as an ugly, snarling head of a dire wolf. There is nothing on the walls here. But a black bearskin rug lies on the bed, and it is well known that Julian sleeps under it whenever he is here.

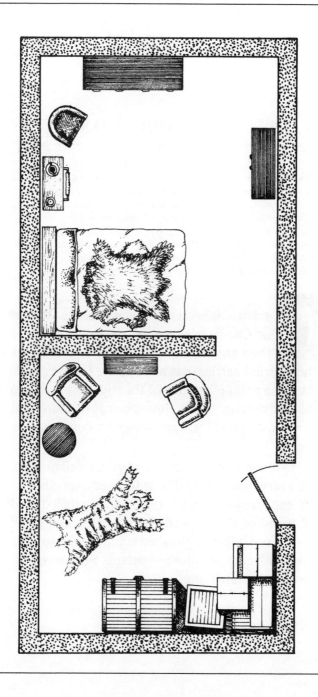

GERARD'S APARTMENTS

"And a big powerful man regarded me from the next card. He resembled me strongly, save his jaw was heavier, and I knew he was bigger than I, though slower. His strength was a thing out of legend. He wore a dressing gown of blue and gray clasped about the middle with a wide, black belt, and he stood laughing. About his neck, on a heavy cord, there hung a silver hunting horn. He wore a fringe beard and a light mustache. In his right hand he held a goblet of wine. I felt a sudden affection for him. He was Gerard." (from Corwin's Chronicles)

erard is as loyal and as steadfast a protector as Castle Amber could ever want. More than anyone else he seemed to rise above the internal battles that marked the Interregnum. At some point every one of the royals has tried to take advantage of his slow generous nature, but somehow Gerard always seems to come out on top.

His chambers reflect his physical orientation. On entry, one's attention is focused immediately on the dragon's head that hangs stuffed and mounted on the far wall. With its gold and green scales, and its huge, polished teeth, the dragon has been captured in a pose of attack. Seen at night, the thing is terrifying.

The rest of the sitting room is unremarkable. The bookshelf contains no books, only mementoes from hunts and battles. And one peculiar item, a Crimson Tide football sweater from Gerard's college days at Alabama. According to him, he was a first-string fullback, but Corwin, who understands football better than most of us, claims he researched the matter and discovered that Gerard was a defensive tackle. Whichever, Alabama did well with him in the line-up.

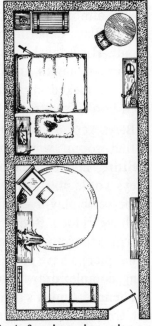

Less than completely tidy, Gerard keeps things scattered throughout his bed-room. Currently it is neat, except for a rumpled bed, a pair of heavy boots on the throw-rug beside the bed, and a sword on the floor, half under the bed. A fencing visor sits on his dresser, and a variety of lances hang on the walls around the room. In the corner, a heavy wooden table is clear.

BLEYS'S APARTMENTS

"Then came a fiery bearded, flame-crowned man, dressed all in red and orange, mainly of silk stuff, and he held a sword in his right hand and a glass of wine in his left, and the devil himself danced behind his eyes, as blue as Flora's, or Eric's. His chin was slight, but the beard covered it. His sword was inlaid with an elaborate filigree of a golden color. He wore two huge rings on his right hand and one on his left: an emerald, a ruby, and a sapphire, respectively. This, I knew, was Bleys." (from Corwin's Chronicles)

leys's rooms are as sparse as Julian's, and almost as messy as Brand's. Like Brand, Bleys experimented with magic and the occult. His bookshelves are lined with books on all sorts of magics, and it has long been suspected that the locked chest in the bedroom contains spell-books from many Shadows.

Bleys kept a chessboard in the corner of the sitting room, where he played with Corwin, Deirdre, and Eric. When no one was around, Bleys would play with people in Shadow, in a sort of perverse play-by-mail arrangement. He claims to have ridden Bobby Fischer's famous queen sacrifice to victory against Fischer himself, but he is happier to have played Tlingel the unicorn to a long, complex draw. Once, while he was drunk, he challenged Amber's own Unicorn to a match, but the Unicorn chose to ignore him.

Two long bookshelves are stuffed with books, manuscripts, and papers on all subjects. Many are occult or magic-based, but others reflect Bleys's fascination with the military, especially the navy.

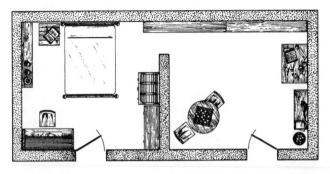

Others deal with heraldry, weapons design and decoration, and ship construction. Among Bleys's interests was the age of the Vikings, and in his tipsier moods he walked the castle at night, shouting at the top of his lungs that the ghost of Eric the Red walked Amber's hallways. Eric the Brother took offense, and Bleys sank even lower in the future king's estimation. But it was funny, and the castle needed it.

We have not identified or traced all of Bleys's magical items. Many of the substances are straightforward, but his spell-books are often arcane and linguistically impenetrable. He seems to have planned his assault on the castle with the help of Shadow-magic, but Corwin's presence probably did as much to hinder as help him. Far more pragmatic than his red-haired brother, Corwin emphasized weapons, numbers, and strategy much more than magic. It's quite possible that Corwin inadvertently stopped Bleys's magical plans.

BENEDICT'S APARTMENTS

"Then there was Benedict, tall and dour, thin; thin of body, thin of face, wide of mind. He wore orange and yellow and brown and reminded me of haystacks and pumpkins and scarecrows and the Legend of Sleepy Hollow. He had a long strong jaw and hazel eyes and brown hair that never curled. He stood beside a tan horse and leaned upon a lance about which was twined a rope of flowers. He seldom laughed. I liked him." (from Corwin's Chronicles)

everal of the royals' apartments are decorated around a particular motif, but only Benedict's takes its entire decor from a specific Shadow. Reflecting his fascination with things Japanese, Benedict has imported all his apartments' furnishings from pre-nineteenth century Japan of Shadow Earth. He carries the stylings out north of the castle, where he has established a thriving Japanese garden.

On entering the room, visitors are expected to remove their shoes. Japanese mats are on the floor, with a paper curtain that slides back to reveal the bedroom. Along the walls in both rooms hang Japanese weapons of all kinds. Shuriken are ordered above the bookcase, while nunchaku hang by their chains over the bed. Other weapons include the No-dachi, the tanto, the katana, and the wakizashi.

The interesting part about Benedict's decor is how well it fits his personality. During the intrigues of the Interregnum, Benedict tried his best to stay away, but when Amber itself became threatened he did what he considered honorable and returned to the castle to help. In the past years he has refrained from battle unless drawn into it, and increasingly his concern is not for the individual but rather for the culture of the Shadow in which he rules. He normally does rule, wherever he travels. He is simply that sort of man.

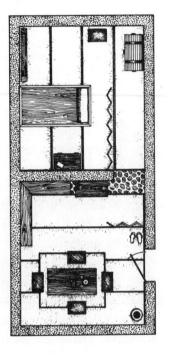

In his bookcases are books untranslated from the Japanese. Haiku, novels, books of strategy and of warfare, books on the emperor and his simultaneous role as ruler and god — these are the things Benedict has become enthralled with. His apartments are utterly fascinating, because of their total surrender to a culture in which he was not raised. By now, Benedict is an Amberite only when Amber is threatened.

"Then there was Eric. Handsome by anyone's standards, his hair was so dark as to be almost blue. His beard curled around a mouth that always smiled, and he was dressed simply in a leather jacket and leggings, a plain cloak, high black boots, and he wore a red sword belt bearing a long silvery saber and clasped with a ruby, and his high collar round his head was lined with red and the trimmings of his sleeves matched it. His hands, thumbs hooked behind his belt, were terribly strong and prominent. A pair of black gloves jutted from the belt near his right hip. He it was, I was certain, that had tried to kill me on that day I had almost died. I studied him and I feared him somewhat." (from Corwin's Chronicles)

ric's apartments are down the hallway from the entrance to the library. Like the chambers of Brand, Bleys, Caine, and Llewella, Eric's have been left intact from the last moments he spent in them. They show signs that he had left hurriedly, but for the most part they are neat and accessible.

Eric's desk-table sits on a round, thick rug on the north wall of the sitting room. Beside it, a bookshelf holds volumes of political and military strategy, and papers which appear to be his own memoirs. These are yet to be examined. Another bookshelf, in the far corner of the sitting room, contains a wealth of volumes about history, novels of historical romance, and a collection of Machiavelli and Locke. Eric was well-read, but often he did not let his intelligence rule him.

On the wall into the bedroom hangs a mace, and a six-foot broadsword is set at an angle on the wall

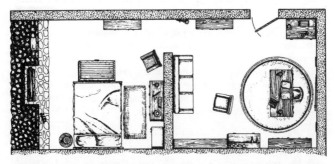

above the bed. The rest of the bedroom is uneventful, with one exception. Of all of us, Eric is the only one who managed to get a room with a fireplace. Had I not already finished my own apartments, I would have taken his after his death, perhaps even before. I like fireplaces, and it was with regret that I agreed with the carpenters that I could not have one in my own rooms. How Eric got one is a mystery to all.

Corwin's chronicles paint a highly unflattering picture of Eric. He and Corwin always fought, and Llewella and I used to place bets on which would kill the other first. It is somehow typical of the royal family that Eric died not in a fratricide, but rather fighting for Amber on the same side as his most hated brother. That he surrendered the Jewel of Judgment to Corwin, whom he despised, is as great a testament as any to his true greatness.

Even more than my other fallen siblings, I pray for Eric that he rest in peace. He was our king, if only for a short time.

"We were in the library, and I was seated on the edge of the big desk. Random occupied a chair to my right. Gerard stood at the other end of the room, inspecting some weapons that hung on the wall. Or maybe it was Rein's etching of the Unicorn he was looking at. Whichever, along with ourselves, he was also ignoring Julian, who was slouched in an easy chair beside the display cases, right center, legs extended and crossed at the ankles . . ." (from Corwin's Chronicles)

he library occupies most of the west wall of the second floor. Usually it is a place of relaxation and study for the members of the royal family. At times, however, it has been a meeting place during periods of greatest crisis. It was here that Brand was rescued from his prison in Shadow during the final days of the Interregnum.

A double door swings inwards from the corridor. A large shelf divides the north from the south portion of the room. On the west (outside) wall, a large marble fireplace burns throughout the winter, frequently even on a cool summer's evening. Like all castles Amber's tends to be cold and damp in humid weather, and the library fireplace is a favorite location for warming one's self.

The library is quite sparsely furnished. Two tall stacks extend out from the southeast wall, three from the north wall. A desk is in the center of the north section, and a larger double table sits under the southwest windows. Smaller shelves and smaller tables line the west wall. A sofa and chair welcome library patrons to sit with their books in front of the roaring flame.

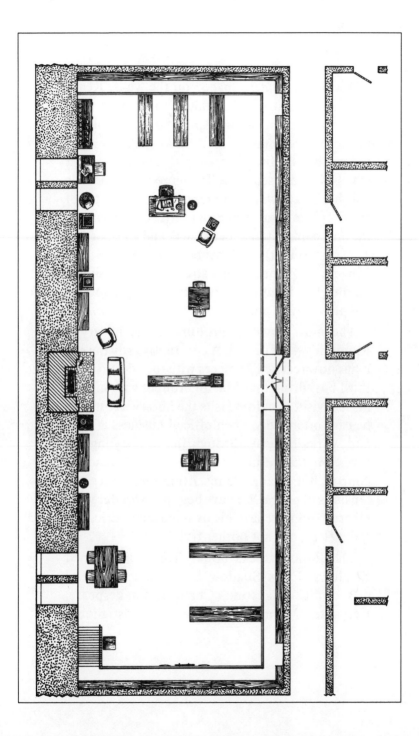

Artwork is widely spaced on the walls. Rein's etching of the Unicorn hangs on the south wall, with swords from various Amberian battles placed attractively around it. A Picasso sketch rests to the south of the fireplace, a small painting beside it which would resemble a Turner except it depicts another Shadow. A long tapestry to the north of the fireplace is an Amberian artist's rendering of the final confrontation between Brand and Corwin. The east (inner) wall bears a Monet and two Eregnorian paintings of a strangely impressionist nature. Far from beautiful, the two Eregnorians are provocative and unusual.

The most obvious furniture in the library is Random's set of drums. A constantly growing set, it has now reached 24 pieces with the addition of a third bass drum that Martin brought with him on his last visit. Random visits the library as often as he can, often daily when official business allows, and works his way through the jazz stylings he loves. At these times it's impossible to read, of course, but Vialle claims drumming eases the tensions of office. We have begun to wonder what Oberon did to relieve his own tensions. Eric, it is quite clear, did not bother trying.

The library stocks books from many varied Shadows. From Shadow Earth come complete sets of St. Augustine, Chaucer, Shakespeare, Cervantes, Montaigne, Machiavelli, Castiglione,

Sidney, Bacon, Ben Jonson, Samuel Johnson, Hegel, Heidegger, Newton, Einstein, Pope, Boccaccio, Milton, Rabelais, and Virgil. Smatterings of Homer, Aristotle (including the lost *Treatise on Comedy*), Juvenal, Aristophanes, Dickens, Faulkner, Dante, Goethe, Proust, Joyce, and Hawthorne are present in their first editions. An entire shelf is devoted to unicorn lore, including an obscure volume entitled *Unicorn Variations,* whose origins remain unknown. Also included is the five-volume truncation of Corwin's Chronicles, which the madman Roger claims to have authored. Filled with colloquialisms of contemporary Shadow Earth, all of us find it difficult to follow. About the crisis, though, it is unexpectedly perceptive.

The ceiling of the library rises to the top of the third floor. From that floor we will look through the windows down into it. From this floor, a set of stairs in the library's southwest corner leads up to a walkway that extends around the perimeter. This walkway has never been used for anything, but as children we would often play on it. It is a mystery that we didn't break our necks.

THIRD FLOOR
CASTLE AMBER

ost of the third floor remains undeveloped. Some of it, in fact, is sealed off. To these sealed-off sections Random has the only key, and the only official access. If they contain things or information the rest of the Amberites should know about, he has yet to explain it to them. There is a strong possibility he hasn't entered these sections at all.

Although the third floor contains five points of interest, only two offer more than a perfunctory exploration. These two are Random's apartments and my own. Mine are the most recently developed, and are therefore quite naturally the most attractive. We will come to them last; from their windows we will look out over the city, and bring our visit to a close.

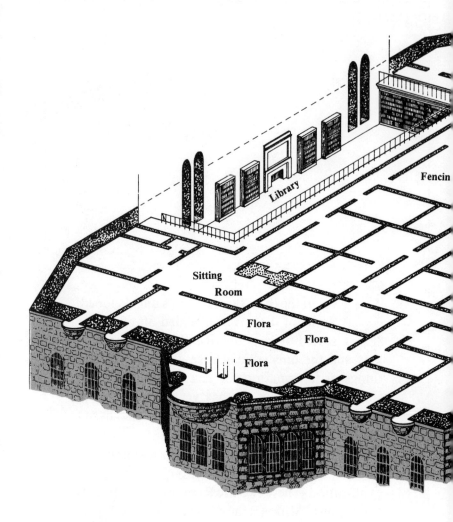

Note: Unmarked Rooms are:
1. Guest Rooms
2. Storage
3. Sitting Rooms

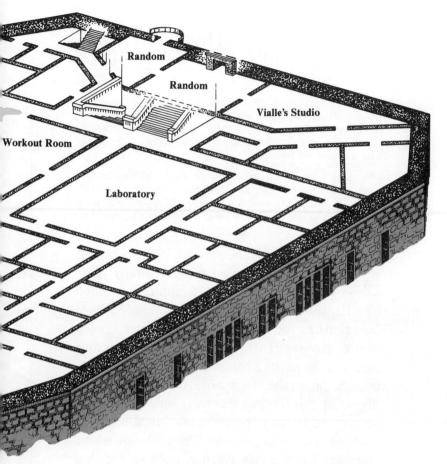

Random

Random

Vialle's Studio

Workout Room

Laboratory

THIRD FLOOR
CASTLE
AMBER

THE APARTMENTS
OF THE KING AND QUEEN

"The one bore a wily-looking little man, with a sharp nose and a laughing mouth and a shock of straw-colored hair. He was dressed in something like a Renaissance costume of orange, red, and brown. He wore long hose and a tight-fitting embroidered doublet. And I knew him. His name was Random."

"I heard her footsteps and then the door swung in. Vialle is only a little over five feet tall and quite slim. Brunette, fine-featured, very soft-spoken. She was wearing red. Her sightless eyes looked through me, reminding me of darkness past, of pain." (from Corwin's Chronicles)

he story of Random and Vialle is one of almost impossible romance. Many years ago, as a young adult, Random descended Faiella-bionin into Rebma. There he met Morganthe, the daughter of Rebma's Queen Moire. He was charming, and she came to love him, and he carried her away from her home. A month later she returned, heartbroken and pregnant. She lived to bear their son Martin, then succumbed to her depression and killed herself.

Much later, Random and Deirdre escorted the amnesiac Corwin into Rebma. Both agreed that Corwin could regain his memory by walking the Pattern, and Rebma's was the only one accessible. But while Corwin was to gain his memory from that trip, Random was to gain a wife. As punishment for his wronging of Morganthe, Moire commanded that he would marry a Rebman subject named Vialle. She was blind and she had

no suitors, and marriage to a prince of Amber, even if he abandoned her a week afterwards, would provide her with an otherwise impossible status. A funny thing happened on the way to the gas chamber: Random and Vialle fell genuinely in love. A funnier thing, especially for a king of Amber, is that Random loves her still. The marriage's success was a surprise to everyone — Random and Vialle included — but it has likely been the strongest single factor behind the current peace of the realm. Random is happy, and he wants all of Amber to know what that means.

The entrance to the king's apartments is the ornate door through the apartment's southeast wall. A wide oaken door, carved with the symbol of the Unicorn offering the Jewel of Judgment, leads into a sitting room where Random receives private visitors. Official audiences take place in the Yellow Room on the ground floor; no state visitor has ever entered the apartments of the King of Amber. Not even Oberon swerved from this policy.

The sitting room is furnished in a style reminiscent of the late medieval period in northern Europe on Shadow Earth. An ancient round table stands in the southeast corner of the room. During dinner visits this will serve as a dining table, but otherwise it remains largely unused. Occupying the northwest quarter of the room is a large table which is used as both desk and dining table as well. On a carpet along the westernmost wall stands a high-backed wooden bench, a rectangular table, two chairs, and a bust of Oberon. The king's chair is obvious; close to the visitors' bench, its high back bears a carving of the crown of Amber. But Random insists it is not a second throne, and has even gone so far as to let his guests sit in it for the entire visit.

The royal couple's bedroom occupies the middle room of their apartments. Its modern decor stands in stark contrast to the venerated medievalism of the sitting room, and it is clear that Random and Vialle redecorated when they moved in. Oberon's furniture was much closer to that of ancient Rome than to anything modern, but Random's long stays in Shadow Earth had given him a different set of tastes.

A sofa and chair wait invitingly along the southern wall, while a desk and chair sit under a

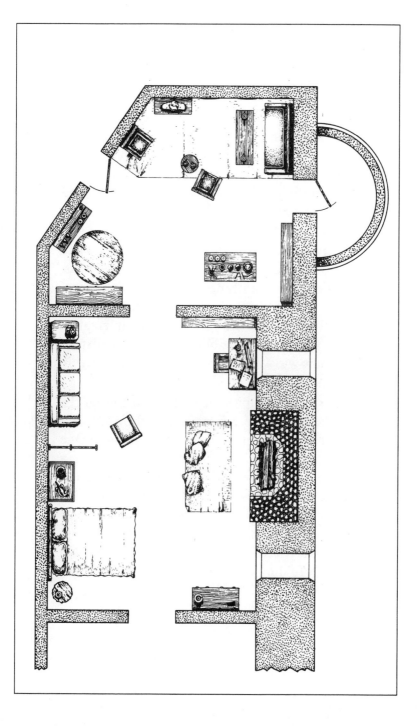

window beside the fireplace. On the table is a document bearing the royal seal, and a quick glance reveals the paper to be an amendment to the Golden Circle treaties. The stone fireplace is large and beautiful; many stories have circulated about the amount of time Random and Vialle spend on the soft rug directly in front of it. I tend not to believe them, however, if only because their big brass bed is just across the room.

In several places within the apartments, small sculptures are placed on tables and mantels. Elegant and brilliantly designed, they are abstractions of several of Amber's royals. Not until recently, however, did we realize their creator. Perhaps because she is blind, we did not suspect that Vialle was a sculptor. She is, and she is highly accomplished.

Her studio occupies the eastern portion of the apartments. Sparsely furnished, it shows several sculptures in various stages of development. One especially notable one, on the rug beneath a window, is a large representation of Random, and somehow Vialle has managed to capture both his seriousness and his insouciance in one superb statue. Her workbench stands beside the rug, while an artist's table touches the southern wall. Behind a folding curtain in the northeast corner are her supplies.

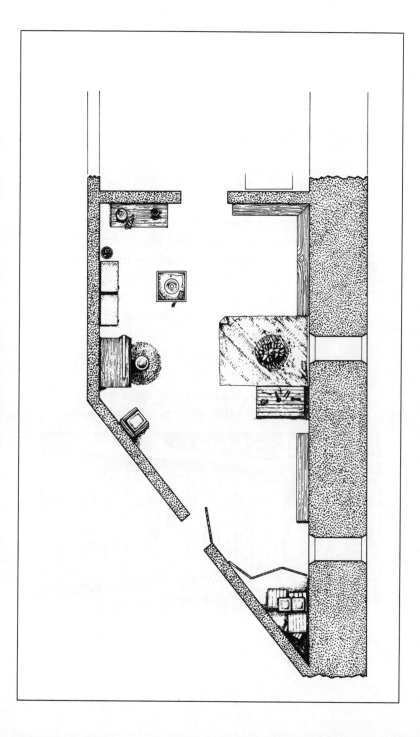

lthough it has not yet been developed, there is a planned entrance to the library from this floor. The library is two stories high, and a walkway runs around the top floor. There are plans to complete this floor, so that more books and manuscripts can be brought in. Random promises this will start next year.

For now, though, all we have is a series of large windows. Through them, the library below looks much less friendly than it really is. Random's drums stick out like a sore thumb, and the shelves

resemble the cold, dusty things found in the universities on almost all Shadows. As an art major at Vassar, I used the library as little as possible, but I remember feeling tired the moment I walked in. Amber's library isn't like that, but through these windows it certainly seems to be.

There is a doorway through the wall, but it is locked. Through it is the walkway that is also accessible by stairs from the bottom floor.

THE FENCING ROOM
AND THE LABORATORY

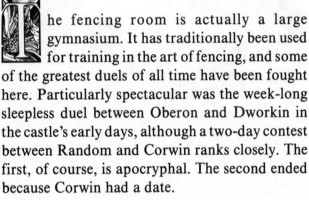

The fencing room is actually a large gymnasium. It has traditionally been used for training in the art of fencing, and some of the greatest duels of all time have been fought here. Particularly spectacular was the week-long sleepless duel between Oberon and Dworkin in the castle's early days, although a two-day contest between Random and Corwin ranks closely. The first, of course, is apocryphal. The second ended because Corwin had a date.

The most noticeable absence in the fencing room is the lack of pure practice weapons. There are no foils here, only a few epees and a wide collection of sabers. Sabering, in fact, is the most common type of fencing, because none of the royals believes in fencing without the threat of death. The epee is used in initial training, but foils are never used at all. According to Eric, who began the system of training Amber's military in the fencing arts, fencing with a foil is like smoking without inhaling: it gives the general idea, but nobody is going to care.

While the lab has been used for a variety of scientific purposes, including Benedict's testing of Prigogine's "Order out of Chaos" thesis, it is primarily a medical treatment center. Five beds line the far wall, desks and cabinets sit against the near wall, and folding curtains lead back towards laboratory tables in the southern section of the room.

Inside the cabinets are surgical instruments, intravenous equipment, microscopes and their associated equipment, and a wide range of first aid materials. All the royals have at one time served in a medical capacity in Shadow, and we have brought what techniques we could back to the castle. Some are chemically impossible, but many have helped. But only the royals and their servants are treated in the castle.

The lab is used almost as commonly to conduct research into poisons. Brand was especially interested in their creation, but Benedict has done some superlative work in antidotes. Other research involves the creation of antibiotics for treating diseases from Shadow. Some of these are extremely difficult to isolate.

Of course, there's always the possibility of bringing chemists from Shadow into the castle. None, however, has been brought from Shadow Earth. Not yet, at least.

FLORA'S APARTMENTS

"The woman behind the desk wore a wide-collared, V-necked dress of blue-green, had long hair and low bangs, all of a cross between sunset clouds and the outer edge of a candle flame in an otherwise dark room, and natural, I somehow knew, and her eyes behind glasses I didn't think she needed were as blue as Lake Erie." (from Merlin's Chronicles)

ast a number of undeveloped or inaccessible areas lie my own apartments. Except for the king's chambers it is the largest of the royal apartments, and unlike the others it was designed especially by the inhabitant, me. The most recent construction in the castle, it was finished during the turmoil of the Interregnum. I guessed, quite rightly, that no one was going to notice.

The entrance, off the northeast wall, sets the tone for the decor that extends throughout. The furniture is French, from the Napoleonic era, because that is the era I love the most. The rug in the sitting room comes from Versailles itself. The portrait of Napoleon, which hangs on the far wall, was commissioned by the emperor as a gift for me. I asked him, for my sake, to keep that ridiculous hat off his head.

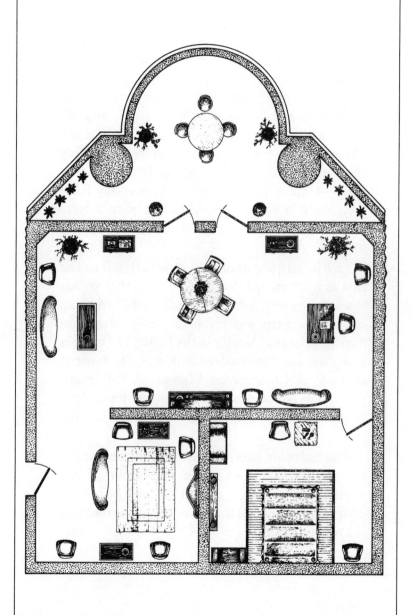

The sitting room leads to my favorite room in the entire palace. Sparely but beautifully furnished, with decor from the same era, it gives me a place where I can stretch out and be entirely myself. The round table in the middle comes from Avignon, while many of the other artifacts are from Nice and Marseilles. A beautiful, brightly colored quill sits on my writing desk, and the tall plants in the corner are full, quickly growing specimens from Eregnor. Along the walls, portraits of many famous men stare moodily from their dark backgrounds; these are men I have known, and I leave to you the ambiguity of that term.

Two items quite naturally attract attention. The first is a stunningly lovely gold harp that stands towards the west side of the room. Of Florencian origin, the harp was given to me by Mussolini during my stay in Venice in the 1930s. The other is a stuffed and mounted white horse, the favorite stallion of Lord Byron himself. A full-length portrait of Byron, his cape melding with the black thunderstorm in the background, hangs on the northern wall.

The bedroom is especially tasteful. The bright red canopied bed occupies the center of the northern wall (beds should be central to all bedrooms). Its sheets are red satin, and its mattress is a feather design from pre-Civil War Charleston.

On the vanity are two exceptional jewels: a diamond necklace from Marie Antoinette, and my favorite curio of all, an authentic, original Fabergé egg. The egg opens to reveal a man and a woman in the throes of passion. It was Fabergé's finest effort by far.

Back through the large room to the doors in the southern wall. These doors lead to a large, semi-circular balcony that overlooks the city of Amber. Plants line the walls and stand on either side of a round table and round chairs that come from my home in Westchester. Often at night I sit at this table, a glass of Napoleon brandy in my hand, and think of the romance that my life has been. I look out over the city, and I think of Amber's people, and I know that their lives can never be even a tenth of that. And then it comes back to me why they worship me as they do.

Come to the windows now, and gaze out over the city.

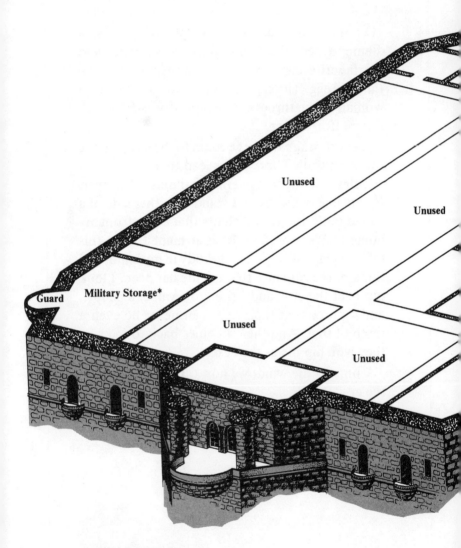

Note: Unmarked Rooms are:
1. Storage
2. Military Storage — supplies
   extra uniforms, etc.

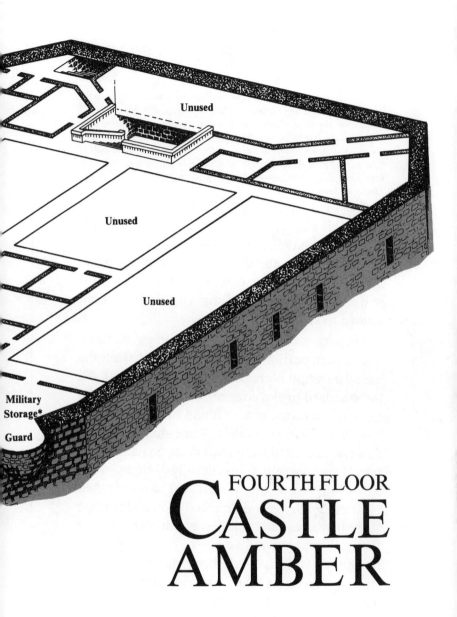

Unused

Unused

Unused

Military
Storage*

Guard

FOURTH FLOOR
CASTLE AMBER

THE CITY OF AMBER

"It was a cool night with the breezed smells of autumn burning down the world about me. I drew it into my lungs and sighed it out again as I headed for the Main Concourse, the distant, almost-forgotten, slow clopping sounds of hoofs on cobbles coming to me like something out of dream or memory. The night was moonless but filled with stars, and the Concourse below flanked by globes of phosphorescent liquid set atop high poles, long-tailed mountain moths darting about them." (from Merlin's Chronicles)

t is afternoon, so Amber is entirely visible. Even at night, however, and even from this distance, the city sparkles from the lights in the phosphorescent globes. From my balcony it is quite beautiful, as all my visitors have been known to say.

The city is divided into two primary sections. The eastern portion is mostly residential, while the western section is predominantly commercial. All the standard professions of Shadow Earth of the early Renaissance can be found here: carpenters, fishers, milliners, clothiers, stone-masons, brick-makers, and artists and craftsmen, to name but a few. House construction is usually of stone, brick, or wood, with the occasional whitewashed plastered wall, the odd thatched roof, and the rare stone mansion, and the tallest buildings have three floors. Shopkeepers live above their shops, and hostels of various kinds keep the poor off the streets. Despite its relative wealth, Amber has its inevitable share of poverty. Temples exist in the

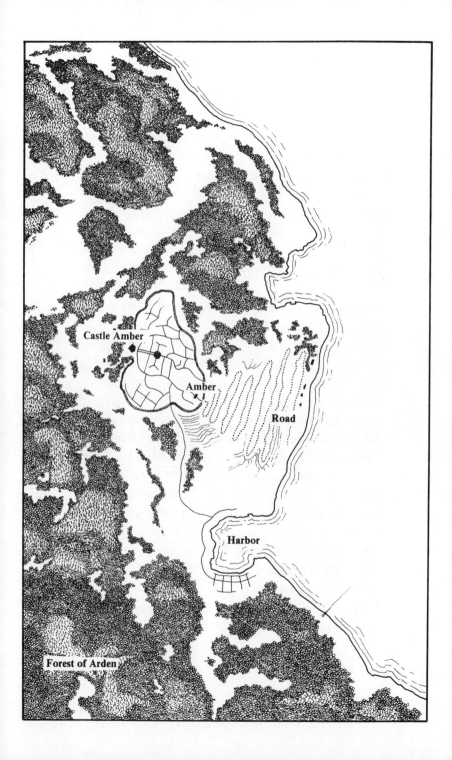

city, but for the most part they are found in the countryside. The Unicorn has never been seen in the city itself, and these sightings determine where the temples are located.

"When I reached the avenue I strolled. A few closed carriages rolled by as I passed along the way. An old man walking a tiny green dragon on a chain leash touched his hat to me as I passed and said, 'Good evening.' He had seen the direction from which I had come, though I was sure he did not recognize me" (that's from Merlin's Chronicles).

Many of the shops, cafes, and restaurants occupy the Main Concourse. A wide cobblestone street, it is the place of business for most Amber merchants. A quick stroll down the Concourse in the middle of the day will reveal deals being made, goods being purchased, and merchants trying to shout their advertisements. At night the cafes and the restaurants remain open until well after dark, sometimes till midnight during feast days. On a warm summer's night I walk there myself some-times, and the people line the Concourse to get to see a member of the family. I go there not for me but for them; a royal visit draws them together. Despite their proximity to the castle, Amberites are really no different from the subjects of any significant kingdom.

Vine Street intersects the Main Concourse and cuts across the city from west to east. On its eastern portion reside many of Amber's nobles, while to the west it leads down to the port district. And "down" is the precise word. To get to the port district means a walk down cobbled streets to where the lights are much further apart and walking much more dangerous. There is something almost archetypal about unsafe harbor areas, and Amber's fits the archetype well. At one point, in fact, Harbor Road gives way to a stretch called Death Alley. All port cities seem to have such a street.

"That was it, the stretch commonly called Death Alley. I turned there. It was just a street like any other. I didn't see any corpses or even collapsed drunks for the first fifty paces, though a man in a doorway tried to sell me a dagger and a mustachioed stock character offered to fix me up with something young and tight. I declined both, and learned from the latter that I wasn't all that far from Bloody Bill's. I walked on. My occasional glances showed me three dark-cloaked figures far to the rear which, I supposed, could be following me; I had seen them back on Harbor Road too. Also, they might not. In that I was not feeling particularly paranoid, I reflected that they could be anybody going anywhere and decided to ignore them. Nothing happened. They kept to themselves, and when I finally located Bloody Bill's and entered, they passed on by, crossing the street and going into a small bistro a little farther along down the way" (from Merlin's Chronicles too).

Predictably, the beer-houses and bars near the harbor are unsavory and dangerous. They also serve the best seafood in the city. Here are made deals of a different order from those made on the Concourse, and here the thieves, the dishonest merchants, and the prostitutes stalk anyone who ventures into the area.

Bloody Bill's is the most popular bar in that district, and the history of its name reveals much about the area. At one time, it was called Bloody Tom's and owned by a man named Sam. When Sam was knifed to death in a fight over an unpaid bill, his son Bill took it over and held it for several years under the name of Bloody Sam's. Recently, Bill was himself stabbed to death, although this time for no apparent reason, and his cousin Andy stepped in to run the place. It is now called Bloody Bill's. The pattern is clear; one wonders what it was called before Tom had it.

"The four of us strode back towards Harbor Street. Interested bystanders got out of our way quickly. Someone was probably already robbing the dead behind us. Things fall apart; the center cannot hold. But what the hell, it's home." Don't you think Merlin writes beautifully?

It's home, and there's more to it. Up from the harbor district, the Concourse swings southeast-

112

wards and then eastwards, marking the boundaries of the city. The southernmost part of the city merges with the trees that lead eventually into forest and out into the countryside. Before it becomes forest, however, some of the finest homes in the city come into view. These are recently built, the result of the nobles' growing dissatisfaction with the invasion by the merchant class of the eastern side of the city. The east still holds its noble houses, but well-constructed row houses are encroaching on what was once exclusive property. The nobles, tired of fighting their years-long battle, have given in and begun to move out. Many still remain, though, refusing to abandon the mansions their families have held for centuries.

Off to the east of the Concourse, but still close to the city's center, is Temple Street. Once the home of the major temples, before the Pureness movements forced them to the countryside, Temple Street has now become the place of entertainment and the arts and crafts. The established theater on the street is called The Crown, because its pentagonal shape is shaped after the crown of Amber (and the outer walls of the castle). Recently its monopoly has been challenged by a rather radical theater group calling themselves the Players of the Unicorn. Unlike the Crown's Company, this new troupe often features excellent roles for women, and admission prices are less than half those of The

Crown. They also strive for spectacle, which The Crown seems to think is inappropriate. Naturally, I have seen fit to become a benefactor of the new theater. Just as naturally, Benedict supports the old.

Temple Street is extremely busy during the long days of summer. Everywhere, visitors pose for portrait-painters, while musicians stroll the narrow street playing their lutes and their guitars or singing songs of the sea. Craftsmen advertise their wares in long, loud shouts, and silent dancing troupes entertain with the hopes of raising enough money to keep their small business alive. Then, suddenly, in the middle of it all, the horns summon the playgoers to The Crown; before they get there, though, they must pass through placard-bearing members of the Unicorn troupe, the placards pleading with them to visit the new theater instead. It is bustling and it is noisy, but the excitement is always high.

This is the street, too, where one finds the best china and the most unusual tapestries and clothing. Because of the influence of the royal family, who shift from Shadow to Shadow and develop tastes according to their travels, potters, tailors, tapestriers, and artists of all kinds display great eclecticism. Tapestry styles range from Anglo-Saxon to eighteenth-century Italian, and even into American and Begman. Fashion is frequently of

Earth's medieval-style — men with long robes of velvet, caps of black velvet, tunics of various colors complete with slashed sleeves and padded shoulders; women in hennin with a trail of gold-colored linen, full trains on low-cut gowns — but fashion is moving recently towards the less elaborate styles reminiscent of eighteenth-century England and France. The variety in styles gives Temple Street a richness that spills into the city as a whole.

The harbor, despite its danger, offers some of the most fascinating activity in the city. The harbor is dotted with warehouses both small and large, with more under construction at almost all times. Ships of nearly 100 tons dock for days, unloading or loading goods, and when they raise their sails to pull away from Amber they catch the gleam of the rising sun in an indescribably beautiful way. Smaller craft sail among the islands, and large ships tow barges full of Shadow wares between the docks. Shipbuilders too, show their works proudly, and the navy of Amber is by far the strongest navy in the Golden Circle. When Caine was alive the navy held semi-yearly naval exercises, and at these times the people of Amber were treated to a truly remarkable sight.

Like its royal family, Amber is eclectic. Influenced by Shadow and by the Golden Circle kingdoms with which it holds trade treaties, it has managed to assimilate a great many different cultures and take the best from each. To many visitors the city seems haphazard and out of control, but this opinion is held in Amber only by the most traditional of the nobles. To them, the Golden Circle treaties were a mistake, because by signing them Amber signed away its uniqueness. But since the signing Amber has seen its greatest activity and its greatest wealth, and what culture it has lost it has replaced with the culture it has learned to share with its neighbors. In other words, Amber has grown much more metropolitan. Most of us in the castle see this as an extremely positive development.

The tour is finished now. It is time for you to leave. Certainly you must have many unanswered questions, but I have appointments in Shadow that I have no choice but to keep. Perhaps you will visit another time, and then your tour guide will tell you the things I missed.

There are many ways to learn more about Amber. The first is to read the Chronicles of Corwin and of Merlin. The best rendering of Corwin's Chronicles can be found in the books called *Nine Princes in Amber*, *The Guns of Avalon*, *Sign of the Unicorn*, *The Hand of Oberon,* and *The Courts of Chaos.* An author from Shadow Earth, who signs himself Roger Zelazny, reputedly received the information for these books from Corwin himself. Merlin's story has been told by the same author, in three books entitled *Trumps of Doom*, *Blood of Amber*, and *Sign of Chaos*. His story remains unfinished. Zelazny himself seems to have authorized two other books, *Seven No-Trump* and *The Black Road War,* but these volumes have not found their way into the castle. I have heard the tale of their authorization, and it seems entirely apocryphal.

There is another way. Apparently, your Shadow is now in possession of a colorful volume called a *Visual Guide to Castle Amber.* The back portion of this book, from what I can surmise, consists of several essays about Amber, drawn from the two Chronicles and from conversations with this Zelazny person. Should you find the book, certainly read it yourself, but please be so kind as to send a copy to me. If it is good, I will place it on our library shelves. If not, I will feed it to the manticore. What it tells about the castle itself I will find extremely interesting. I only hope that it remembers to mention me.

And now, I must leave you. Remember me, and remember Amber as well. It is not a place you will easily forget.

THE GREATER TRUMPS

"They were almost lifelike in appearance, the Greater Trumps ready to step right out through those glistening surfaces. The cards seemed quite cold to my touch, and it gave me a distinct pleasure to handle them. I had once had a packet like this myself, I suddenly knew." (from Corwin's Chronicles)

ard games have been popular in our culture for a long time, and very few people have not played with a deck of cards at some point in their lives. Even our language reflects the ubiquitous nature of cards, with casual conversation using such metaphors as "I aced the exam" or "He's the joker in the deck." "He's not playing with a full deck" is only one of the less fortunate sayings.

For most people, cards are a pleasant pastime. For some, though, they're a way of life. Gamblers live with their cards, bridge players spend untold hours studying them, and Tarot experts earn their keep by reading people's fortunes.

For the royal family of Amber, their deck of cards is life itself.

Each of the royals has a deck, or can at least make use of another's. Some of the cards are of lesser importance — the wands, pentacles, cups, and swords that make up the more familiar Tarot decks. But each deck contains a group of cards distinguished from the others in one important way: on the faces of these cards are lifelike paintings of the members of the Amber royal family. Let Corwin describe what one looks like:

"Then came a fiery bearded, flame-crowned man, dressed all in red and orange, mainly of silk stuff, and he held a sword in his right hand and a glass of wine in his left, and the devil himself danced behind his eyes, as blue as Flora's, or Eric's. His chin was slight, but the beard covered it. His sword was inlaid with an elaborate filigree of a golden color. He wore two huge rings on his right hand and one on his left: an emerald, a ruby, and a sapphire, respectively. This, I knew, was Bleys."

As with so many other things in Amber, the Greater Trumps are works of living art. Art not in the still-life sense, nor in the sense of the abstract, but rather art that captures the mind and the emotions, that allows the observer to enter inside and see that the art is alive. Like the eyes of the Mona Lisa. Like the grandeur of the Sistine Chapel.

Through the Greater Trumps, the royal family keeps contact with each other. Like a telephone, they permit conversations at long distances. But they are much more than a simple telephone. First, the conversations can cross the boundaries of Shadows. Second, the Trumps do more than transmit words. They also transport people.

To use a Trump for conversation, the "caller" focuses his attention on the picture on the card. If he focuses hard enough, and if the person in the picture is able to receive that focus, contact is made between the two people. After they converse, they pass a hand over the face of the card to break contact.

To use a Trump for transportation, the two Amberites follow the same procedure. Once verbal contact is established, though, they try for a physical contact as well. The caller perceives the card with his full concentration, then reaches his hand through it and towards the receiver's outstretched hand. When the two hands meet, the receiver pulls the caller through. The two royals are now physically side by side. This is known as "Trumping in."

Often the contact is weak. When this happens, the caller has two choices. He can either increase his concentration, or he can ask for help. The only people qualified to help him, unfortunately, are others who know how to use the Trumps. In other words, the rest of the royal family, or a very few others. But rarely will the royals cooperate in a combined contact of this kind — the rescue of Brand remains one of the few occasions — and even more rarely will the caller want the rest of the family to know what he's trying to do. So combined contact doesn't happen very often.

The only difference between a Greater Trump and an ordinary playing card is the sensation of temperature. But there is no actual temperature difference, just the sensation of one. In order to use the card, the caller must feel its coolness, even though the card itself is not actually cool. Knowing that sensation is part of the Amberites' training; they must learn to feel the Trumps just as they must learn to feel the shifting of Shadows. Both are part of their education in perception.

The Trumps are focusers: nothing more and nothing less. Created originally by Dworkin, their artwork is so vivid that they allow the Amberite to fully recall the features of the royal he is trying to contact. Strictly speaking, the cards themselves aren't necessary for this contact, but without them contact is much, much more difficult. While in his cell, in fact, Corwin tried to contact some of the others while only imagining the Trumps (he was blind and the cell was dark), but he failed. Of course, those who were nearby would likely have refused the contact anyway. Refusal is always possible.

Truly effective use of the Greater Trumps comes only after the user has walked the Pattern. The Pattern both demands and teaches super-human concentration, and only with such power of focusing can an Amberite use Trump contact at any distance whatever. Trumps can be devised by any skilled artist though (as Merlin finds out in *Trumps of Doom,*), so their use is far from restricted. In fact, as Bill Roth explains in *Trumps of Doom*, they are made by "a number of experts in the Courts of Chaos," and by "Fiona and Bleys back in Amber." Artists outside of Amber could create them, but they would be imperfect. Doing a perfect set requires walking the Pattern in Amber or the Logrus in Chaos.

Like everything else to come out of Amber, the Trumps are as dangerous as they are helpful.

BENEDICT

ith his almost obsessive belief in the cerebral, Benedict is probably the most reliable of all the Amberites. He despises the family's constant bickering, and he has tried over the years to stay out of it completely. His interests lie with the mind rather than the emotions, as reflected by his fascination with games of pure strategy and his growing assimilation of traditional Japanese customs. He will help if he is needed, but he prefers to be left to himself.

BLEYS

As fiery as the color of his hair, Bleys was the family's most fun-loving member. But his brand of fun was far from clean or pure, as his scheming mind plotted embarrassment after rich embarrassment for the members of the family who took themselves most seriously. For much of his life he despised seriousness, yet when Eric reached for the throne Bleys changed dramatically. At that moment he sought to save Amber, perhaps installing himself as king in the process, and suddenly his mission became highly serious. He failed, of course, dying in the battle at Corwin's side, but Random has not let his efforts be forgotten.

BRAND

Brand was the villain of the piece in the Chronicles of Corwin. He tried to re-draw the Pattern of Amber, thereby giving himself the power almost of a creator. Corwin thwarted him, recasting the Pattern himself. As far as is known, Brand died with the defeat. In life he was moody and sullen, and he faced his tasks with a stubborn determination. Once set on a course of action he was loath to change it, and the courses he chose were rarely less than globally significant. Powerful and brooding, he was among the most romantic of the entire Amberite clan.

CAINE

Strong in body and mind, Caine was something of a soothing presence in the Amberian court. He was able to joke about the royals' hatred for one another, and he often cast himself in the role of a rake for the sake of diverting his brothers' anger to himself. But he was headstrong as well, not trusting any prince he believed had acted against Amber. He was prepared to fight any who threatened the throne. His loyalty to Amber, however well he tried to disguise it, makes his death that much harder to accept.

CORWIN

he narrator of the first five Amber books, Corwin was Oberon's choice for next King of Amber. After his capture by Eric, in fact, Corwin crowned himself king, albeit mainly to disrupt Eric's own coronation. By the end of his war with Brand, though, Corwin no longer wanted the throne, and he welcomed the Unicorn's selection of Random for the kingship. This confirmed that Corwin had changed in the course of his Chronicles from an impetuous, selfish man to a true prince of Amber. In the end, he alone saved Amber from destruction. At present, his whereabouts are completely unknown.

DALT

Humorless and tough, Dalt suits very well his image as a cold-blooded professional mercenary. Dalt's mother, a militant religious fanatic responsible for the desecration of various Unicorn shrines throughout Amber and adjacent Shadows, was defeated and raped by Oberon. She died fighting Bleys years later. Dalt holds a very strong grudge against Oberon and he has vowed to destroy Amber as an act of vengeance for his mother's humiliation.

DARA

erlin's mother and Corwin's mate, Dara is stubborn, willful, and ingenious. Even with their enormous differences she remains fond of Corwin, and although she refuses to admit it, she is suspected to be searching for him on her own. The feeling in the Courts of Chaos is that if anyone finds him it will be her. Tied to rationality much less than the Amberites, and yet understanding Corwin's inborn dependence on reason, she is able to spring free from traditional thought and figure things out in a wholly unique manner. Given Corwin's state of mind at the end of his war with Brand and Chaos, this unique mindset seems necessary if she is to find him. What she wants from him remains to be determined.

DEIRDRE

As beautiful as her name, Deirdre was perhaps the family's greatest loss during the war against Brand. Continually caught in the midst of the most bitter in-fighting, her desire to stabilize the volatile situation kept her from backing away from any of her brothers' battles. Her death was the result of her willingness to help. When she died, something of the royals' greatness died with her. To the people of Amber she was almost a goddess, strong and kind and lovely beyond words.

ERIC

The only King of Amber to die in battle, Eric spent most of his adult life figuring out how to get the throne. He was rash and scheming, Machiavellian to an extreme, and he refused at all times to surrender. Determination of this intensity has its price, of course, and for Eric that price was a paranoia that bordered on the psychotic. His hatred of Corwin was probably the strongest hatred in the Amber royal family; eventually it led to his rashest act of all, his self-coronation as King of Amber. That act, more than any other, spelled his defeat. On the field of death, however, he proved his love for Amber by giving the powerful Jewel of Judgment, the only thing that could save Amber, to his most hated enemy.

FIONA

Recently more active than ever in the affairs of Amber, with her interest in Merlin, Fiona has begun to know the problems of Amberian intrigue. Sarcastic, witty, and capable of unbelievable obnoxiousness, Fiona sided against Corwin during the Interregnum but seems to have accepted Random's reign easily. This could be because Random lets her go her own way, but more likely because Corwin's battle against Chaos alerted her to dangers far beyond the Amberian court. Whatever the reason, she is determined to help Merlin in whatever ways she can.

FLORA

er interests are few, having to do mostly with power, wealth, intrigues, and men. She tends to be brash and gaudy, loving of spectacle and a believer in the dictum, "Nothing in moderation." Her greatest fear is simply being on the wrong side. For that reason she changes allegiance quickly and easily, feeling true loyalty towards no one at all. Unlike Fiona she is unconcerned about the exclusively male lineage of the house of Amber, because she wants none of the responsibility of rule.

GERARD

Huge, powerful, and intimidating, Gerard is far less devious than any of his brothers or sisters and he knows his limitations. He is more trusting of the others, and towards Amber he is unquestioningly loyal. Gerard was the one who insisted on caring for Brand until his brother's safety could be guaranteed, and yet he did not hesitate to join Corwin against Brand when the latter's conspiracy could finally be proven. He is for Amber, pure and simple.

JULIAN

His capacity for mischief and hatred is great, but like most of the princes his love for Amber guides his most important actions. His favorite haunt is Arden Forest, which he traverses on his horse Morgenstern. More than anything else he dislikes being beaten at his own game. In this way he is probably the least mature of all the princes. Still, he is an excellent swordsman and cavalryman, and the defense of Amber itself has often fallen into his hands.

L LEWELLA

uiet and calm, Llewella, like Caine, was a stabilizing influence during the chaotic days at the end of the Interregnum. But unlike Caine she was practically uninterested in the affairs of the court itself, preferring her retreats in Shadow to the relentless intrigues that occupied her brothers and sisters. She has continued that pattern ever since, and she seems to have grown tired of the court altogether. She spends nearly all her time away now, in a Shadow where she has taken to the arts and the dance.

LUKE

Nearly a psychological chameleon, Luke possesses the ability to shift roles almost instantly. A California salesman by profession, he swings into his Amber persona effortlessly whenever the occasion demands. Like Merlin, whom he perhaps most resembles, he retains his Earth personality when he travels among Shadow, and this has caused him a needless amount of difficulty. He likes Merlin, and at times sides with him, but just as often he finds himself on the opposite pole. This has created a consistent, respected rivalry between the two. It has also created a distinct amount of fear among the Amberites and the Chaosians: if Luke and Merlin ever team up, they will be a very dangerous pair.

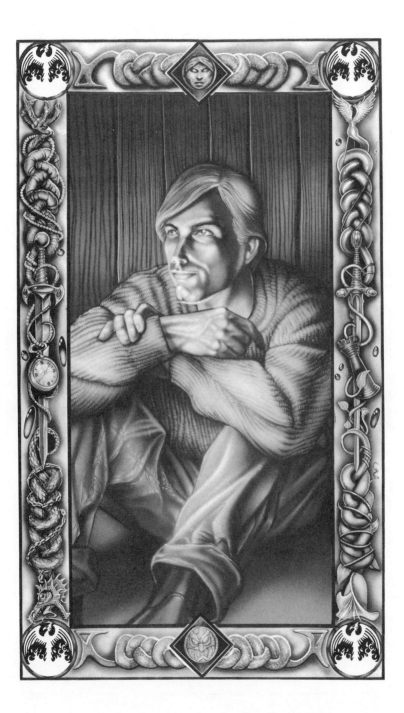

MANDOR

man of considerable talent and knowledge, Mandor seems almost propelled out of Shadow Earth's Italian Renaissance. Capable of plotting and scheming with the best of that era's Machiavelli-inspired politicians, he is capable as well of genuine respect and admiration. Currently, that admiration is for Merlin, his foster brother. Mandor is a complex man, and his role in the current struggle is merely beginning. With his talents, he is likely to make a strong impact.

154

MARTIN

Martin is the son of Random of Amber and Morganthe of Rebma. As Random's son, of course, he is the heir to the throne of Amber, but whether the others would allow this to happen remains entirely to be seen. Tending towards the avant-garde, Martin sports a Mohawk haircut and outlandish (even for Amber) clothes. He drums in a rock fusion band, and has begun to move into the world of computerized music. From observing him, it is clear he has a great deal of maturing to do before he will be given a large role in Amberian affairs. For now, at least, that seems to be the way he wants it.

 **MERLIN**

he son of Corwin of Amber and Dara of Chaos, Merlin was raised in the Courts of Chaos. Shortly before his father's disappearance, he listened to Corwin tell his own story, and since then Merlin has wanted to know more about his father's world. He has spent several years wandering in Shadow, settling for a time on Shadow Earth. Recently he has returned more often to Amber. He is intellectually brilliant and afraid of practically nothing. Still learning of the results of walking both the Pattern of Amber and the Logrus of Chaos, he uses his own powers hesitantly, since nobody in either court can tell him exactly what he might achieve. Like his father he is a superb storyteller, but he lacks Corwin's sense of the personal epic. Perhaps, with age, this will come as well.

RANDOM

The current King of Amber was selected by the Unicorn at the end of Corwin's Chronicles. Something of a renegade, Random's primary interests are women, wine, and song. A prodigious flirt before his marriage to Vialle, he was equally determined to become a first-class jazz drummer. He was never particularly interested in the problems of the succession, staying away from the family's in-fighting until Corwin himself returned to the fray. After that, Random sided with Corwin and proved a significant element in the defeat of Brand. He is extremely happy in his marriage (a rarity for an Amberite), and as a king he is cautious but firm.

VIALLE

andom's queen has done so much to temper the king's impetuosity that she seems fully responsible for his sudden, dramatic maturation. She is quiet about Amberian affairs, preferring to offer instead complete support for Random's actions. She clearly loves her husband, and to the surprise of all, her husband loves her just as strongly. Vialle is blind, and she is a sculptress. Her sculptures boast a simplicity that belies her great personal attention to physical detail, and in this contradiction it seems she has found a unique artistic expression. Through the quietness of her art, and the quietness of her person, Vialle has single-handedly but indirectly altered the atmosphere of Castle Amber. She has no enemies.

OBERON

Not much is known about the father of the current royal family. What is known is told by his children, with all the distortions a child's knowledge of his father is liable to have. Oberon was clearly a firm, demanding father, but just as clearly he had an enormous capacity for teaching his children what he wanted them to learn. He was a superb tactician, both militarily and politically, and with the help of Dworkin he perfected several strategies as well. He loved life almost as much as he loved women, and he loved women almost as much as he loved Amber. In many ways, in fact, Oberon was Amber, and he died heroically to save it.

DWORKIN

Mad, abstract, and totally beyond the realities of even the Amberian royalties, Dworkin is the supreme artist, the artist who can mold reality out of art. Born in Chaos, he escaped to create the Pattern of Amber, thereby giving shape, boundary, line and form to a world that before him had none. In that sense he is a God-figure, a shaper, a maker, "a poietes" in the language of the Greeks. It is said that he was sly and devilish in youth, as scheming and conniving as any of the current Amberites. But to say anyone knows him is a foolish exaggeration.

he Ghostwheel, which Merlin created as a surprise for Random, can probably be described as the ultimate Trump. A supercomputer of the most super kind, it has the ability to search through Shadow and let the user keep track of whatever Shadows he wants. It works by creating the equivalent of Trumps, then searching through them all. By incorporating elements of the Pattern into its design, Merlin gave it the magical qualities it needed to avoid having to make it an initiate of the Pattern or the Logrus.

There is a Trump for the Ghostwheel (Merlin created it), which allows the user to program it from afar. This Trump is a kind of magical remote terminal, and the Ghostwheel responds to the user's spoken commands. Merlin's idea was to give Random that Trump, to let the King of Amber keep an improved watch on Shadows both friendly and enemy. But a problem has surfaced. The Ghostwheel has developed a personality. It didn't like Random's order that Merlin shut it down, and it's not even talking to its creator. Seems Merlin has a few bugs to work out.

SHADOW-SHIFTING AND HELLRIDES

he royal family's most fascinating characteristic is its ability to move from one Shadow to another. At the beginning of *Nine Princes in Amber,* Corwin is in Shadow Earth, and by the end of the *Courts of Chaos* he has traveled to an enormous variety of different Shadows. Like all the royals, his love is for the first Shadow, Amber itself, but he has many connections with many other Shadows as well.

Shadow-shifting is an art. It demands an extremely strong imagination, superhuman powers of perception, and an ability to concentrate absolutely. Of course, not everyone has these capabilities, and that's why the number of Shadow-shifters is so limited. Only the greatest artists of Shadow Earth would have anything approaching these powers, but few of them have ever known the technique.

To start shifting Shadows, the Amberite moves as far as possible from the vicinity of Kolvir. Amber's Shadow-less influence is so strong that successful attempts to Shadow-shift away from Amber itself have been extremely limited. Once away from Kolvir, the shifter focuses his attention on one single feature of the Shadow he's standing in, and tries to perceive of a similar object in the Shadow he seeks. This thing might be a rock, or a twig, or a building, or a book, or a person, but it must be a specific thing, not just a general commodity. If there's nothing in the present Shadow to focus on, he can try to perceive the object in his mind only, but this makes shifting much more difficult. Naturally, the more familiar the shifter is with the Shadow, the more easily he can shift into it.

With the item firmly in mind, the shifter starts moving. He can walk, shifting slowly but safely, or he can run, with his safety a little less certain. More daring souls can copy Random, shifting Shadows while racing along in a Mercedes, and it's even possible to shift while flying a jet fighter. In most Shadows, where this kind of technology is unavailable, the most dangerous shifting of all is performed on a galloping horse. This, we know, is called a hellride. We'll return to those shortly.

As the Amberite moves, he maintains his concentration on the single object. Shortly, he will begin to perceive another object from the desired Shadow. Now, he concentrates on both. As he continues to move, and continues to concentrate, more things from the Shadow come into his mind, until slowly the Shadow begins to take on a defined form. At this point, too, some of the acquired perceptions begin to change, so that they fit more closely to the Shadow as a whole.

Finally, after considerable time and a great deal of movement, the Shadow is complete. Actually, it's not complete until the Amberite is actually in it, because in the original perception he was part of the Shadow. At the same time, though, he cannot become part of that Shadow until he has entirely perceived it. In other words, and this is paradoxical, the Shadow isn't complete until he enters it, and he can't enter it until it's complete.

Of course, this brings up all kinds of philosophical questions, some of which the royal family themselves have tried to solve. The most interesting one is this: does the shifter create the Shadow, or does he simply move to a place that already exists? The question is not really answerable, as Corwin himself explains in *Sign of the Unicorn*:

"Solipsism, I suppose, is where we have to begin — the notion that nothing exists but the self, or, at least, that we cannot truly be aware of anything but our own existence and experience. I can find, somewhere, off in Shadow, anything I can visualize. Any of us can . . . It can be argued, and in fact has, by most of us, that we create the Shadows we visit out of the stuff of our own psyches, that we alone truly exist, that the Shadows we traverse are but projections of our own desires."

By the end of his story, though, Corwin is fairly sure this isn't the case. He's matured considerably by this time, and he wants to believe there's more to reality than the things he and the other royals choose. But the question certainly hasn't gone away, nor will any amount of arguing force it to.

Here's another snag: if the shifter has to concentrate on a specific item from the Shadow, then he'll never be able to travel to a Shadow he knows nothing about. The answer is simple: if he can imagine it, he can travel to it. With nothing concrete for his mind to hold to, the shifter must concentrate fiercely (which stops most from trying it), and with no certainty of the outcome it's extremely dangerous, but it's possible to get to any place inside your imagination. What this means, of course, is that the royalty of Amber could travel, if they wanted, to Middle Earth, Narnia, Pern, or even Utopia.

The problem is, they could get trapped there. Most fictional worlds have some realistic flaw in them, some scientific paradox or impossibility, and the Amberites' physical selves would probably not survive. Or, if they did, they might destroy the fictional world. For these reasons, and also because the royals are too busy plotting and scheming to bother with such experiments, none of them has even tried for a fictional world. Besides, what could they possibly have that Amber or its Shadows don't?

There's another way to get trapped in a Shadow. Shadow-shifting requires light, at least the easiest and safest Shadow-shifting. If there's no light, it's possible to be trapped, because Shadow-shifting from the imagination doesn't always work, and it certainly isn't safe. This is one of the reasons that Eric burned out Corwin's eyes in *Nine Princes in Amber*. When Corwin couldn't see, there wasn't much he could do. Of course, he was also extremely weak, and weakness is another trap. If Eric had wanted to be less cruel, he might have exiled Corwin to a featureless place. With no features to go by, he would have no objects to concentrate on. He would have been forced to shift from the imagination, a dangerous thing to try.

The Amber royals aren't the only ones who can Shadow-shift. As Bill Roth points out to Merlin (in *Trumps of Doom*), Chaosians who have walked the Logrus are able both to move into Shadows and to bring things from Shadows to them. And there are other possibilities as well. Here is his explanation:

"There are a number of magical beings, like the Unicorn, who can just wander wherever they want, and you can follow a Shadow-walker or a magical being through Shadow for so long as you can keep track of it, no matter who you are. Kind of like Thomas Rhymer in the ballad. And one Shadow walker could lead an army through (Corwin and Bleys do this in *Nine Princes in Amber*). And then there are the inhabitants of the various Shadow kingdoms nearest to Amber and to Chaos. Those at both ends breed mighty sorcerers, just because of their proximity to the two power centers. Some of the good ones can become fairly adept at it — but their images of the Pattern or the Logrus are imperfect, so they're never quite as good as the real thing. But on either end they don't even need an initiation to wander on in. The Shadow interfaces are thinnest there. We even have commerce with them."

There may have been a time, in the distant past, when the only Shadow-shifters were Amberites who had walked the Pattern. As in all worlds, and all Shadows, things have changed.

To Shadow-shift quickly, the Amberite hops on a horse. Speeding to a gallop, he picks out his object of concentration and holds the focus as carefully as he possibly can. The destination

Shadow forms quickly, but the danger to the shifter is very, very high. This is the hellride.

The first danger is the horse. It must be trained to keep running no matter what it sees, and not to be distracted. Corwin's Star is trained; few other horses could manage.

The second danger is distraction. During the hellride the shifter sees so much that only the most intense concentration will keep him on course. Who but an Amberite royal, for instance, could refuse to be distracted by this:

"A strong wind . . . Clouds across the stars . . . A bright fork spearing a shattered tree to my right, turning it into flame . . . A tingling sensation . . .The smell of ozone . . . Sheets of water upon me . . . A row of lights to my left . . . Clattering down a cobbled street . . . A strange vehicle approaching . . . Cylindrical, chugging . . . We avoid one another . . . A shout pursues me . . . Through a lighted window the face of a child . . ."

It's impossible not to be distracted, but in *The Courts of Chaos* Corwin manages. If he had stopped to find out about the child, though, he would have been grounded in that Shadow, at least until he started to shift himself out. It would have cost him time, and it might have cost him his life. During *The Courts of Chaos*, in fact, it might have cost him Amber.

To accomplish all this, the hellrider himself must be trained. Because he will be perceiving things at a speed greater than sight can accommodate, he must know how to cultivate a sensation of the destination Shadow. To do so without being distracted by the sensations that come from the interim Shadows is something only a highly experienced shifter could even begin to hope for.

To an observer, the hellrider is merely an apparition. More than one Earth apparition, indeed, has been a hellriding Amberite, and there's a possibility that some UFOs have been objects that have become somehow attached to an Amberite who is hellriding through this Shadow. They appear, and then they disappear, just like the hellrider himself.

One more thing about hellrides. They're disorienting. So much so, in fact, that anyone weaker than a royal of Amber would probably go insane. For this reason, no Amberite tries his first hellride without coaching from another family member. Even for them, that first hellride is exactly as its name suggests: a terrifying, maddening, mind-threatening ride through hell.

SHADOW-STORMS

here are several ways of bringing items from Shadow into Amber. One way, of course, is to have one of the royals carry it with him. Another is through one of the sorcerers of the neighboring Shadows, or with a person who accompanied or followed that royal. The Unicorn, or another free-shifting magical being, might also bring it. Finally, there is the Shadow-storm.

What is a Shadow-storm? Again, Merlin explains: "It's a natural but not too well-understood phenomenon. The best comparison I can think of is a tropical storm. One theory as to their origin has to do with the best frequencies of waves that pulse outward from Amber and from the Courts, shaping the nature of Shadows. Whatever, when such a storm rises it can flow

through a large number of Shadows before it plays itself out. Sometimes they do a lot of damage, sometimes very little. But they often transport things in their progress."

If the Shadow-storm is strong enough, it could pick up not just objects but people as well. Imagine waking up the night after a party, staring at an orange tree against a brilliant green sky, with two armed rodents pointing spears at your forehead. If you lived, you could suggest to Webster's a brand new definition for "hangover."

179

THE PATTERN OF AMBER

he Pattern of Amber lies behind a dark, metal-bound door deep inside Kolvir. Getting there means finding a secret passageway in a corridor inside the walls of the castle. From there, the route leads down a winding stairway of great length, then through a tunnel to the seventh side passage. Finally, it comes to the locked door.

Once through the door, no light is needed. The Pattern casts enough. It appears as an elaborate tracery of bright power, composed mainly of curves, with a few straight lines near the middle. As Corwin tells us, "It reminded me of one of those maze things you do with a pencil, to get you into or out of something." The entire Pattern is

visible from the outside, but it has to be conquered a bit at a time.

Near the corner of the room is the starting point. There, the walker places his foot inside the first set of inlaid lines. Once the walk has begun, there is no turning back.

"It's an ordeal, but it's not impossible or we wouldn't be here. Take it very slowly and don't let yourself be distracted. Don't be alarmed by the shower of sparks that will arise with each step. They can't hurt you. You'll feel a mild current passing through you the whole time, and after a while you'll start feeling high. But keep concentrating, and don't forget — keep walking! Don't stop, whatever you do, and don't stray from the path, or it'll probably kill you."

That's how Random instructed Corwin. And even though the Pattern he was describing was the Pattern below Rebma, all the Patterns seem to affect walkers the same way.

With the first step, blue sparks (blue-white in some instances) outline the foot. A current begins, and soon an audible crackling and a feeling of resistance. Around the first curve, the resistance increases. Here is the First Veil.

If the walker manages to will himself through the First Veil, things get a little easier, at least for a short while. But the Second Veil is more difficult, and by this time the walker's entire being seems to be composed solely of will. Like Shadow-shifting and Trumping, the Pattern requires enormous powers of focus and concentration.

Past the Grand Curve, the route is simply a battle. The Pattern seems to demand sheer determination, and the walker feels his own death and rebirth with virtually every step. But if his will is strong enough he will finally get through, and at last he will pass through the Final Veil.

Then he is in the center.

From the center of the Pattern, an act of will will transport the walker to any place he can visualize. Any Shadow, any place in any Shadow, even a specific room inside Castle Amber. It's possible to simply retrace his steps, but there's no point to this. If, for some reason, he wants to go back to the Pattern's beginning, he need only will himself there.

A person who has successfully walked the Pattern is called an initiate. Initiates gain the knowledge of Shadow-shifting, and they are more adept than others in the use of Trumps. Other powers are suspected, but none have been proven.

The Pattern controls Amber, and thus all of Shadow that Chaos has not taken. Only because of the Pattern's existence has Chaos been kept at bay at all.

THE COURTS OF CHAOS
AND THE LOGRUS

o the royal family of Amber, the Courts of Chaos have long been the enemy. Their existence is seen as the result of the fall of Amber's glory, and all Amberites know they must always guard against Chaos's intrusions. For the common Amberite, though, the Courts are little more than a mysterious legend, and even the royals have a hard time understanding them.

For Corwin's son Merlin, though, the Courts of Chaos are home. At least, one of his homes. Merlin was born in Chaos, the son of Dara of Chaos and Corwin of Amber, and until he listened to Corwin's story he was content to stay in Chaos forever. But he suddenly realized there was more to be seen, so he followed his father's earlier path and went to Shadow Earth. He speaks little of the Courts themselves. What we know from him is that the Courts are a real place, that Chaos is not just an abstraction. Of course, we knew part of this in Corwin's recounting of the battle against Chaos (called the Patternfall Battle). But from Corwin's perspective the Courts were strange; from Merlin's they are far less evil.

While Amber takes its existence from the Pattern, the Courts of Chaos exist through the Logrus. True to its character, the Logrus is not set.

184

Instead, it is more like a maze that shifts unpredictably and dangerously. Walking it is mostly an exercise in trying to stay sane. Once the walk is accomplished, the power of the Logrus resides within the initiate.

To use the power, the initiate must concentrate on the Logrus's form. Or, rather, its formlessness. Once the Logrus is invoked, it can be used in many different ways, depending on the initiate's situation. In *Blood of Amber*, for instance, Merlin uses a Logrus-seeing to spot a hidden door, then extends his Logrus-members to open it. His description gives us a strong sense of Logrus-power:

"I twisted my hand deeper into the Logrus until I wore the limbs I desired as fine-fingered gauntlets, stronger than metals, more sensitive than tongues in the places of their power . . . I summoned more force from the body of the Logrus, which swam specterlike within and before me, and I poured this energy into the gauntlets, the pattern of the Logrus changing form again as I did so."

The Pattern of Amber is a pathway to its own center, but the Logrus of Chaos is a living, swirling, always changing pattern. The Pattern focuses power, but the Logrus extends power. If the Pattern is altered, Amber changes, but change is the first quality of the Logrus. In many ways, the Logrus seems more powerful, more useful, and far more adaptable. Is it any wonder that Amber fears Chaos?

THE JEWEL
OF JUDGMENT

roperty of the Unicorn, the Jewel of Judgment belongs officially to the King of Amber. Eric, at his death, gave the Jewel to Corwin, and eventually the Unicorn gave it to Random. Random possesses it still.

The Jewel is a single huge ruby pendant that hangs on a gold chain around the wearer's neck. To use it necessitates becoming attuned to it. This means wearing it to the center of the Pattern, then holding it up and trying to project one's self inside it. Once attuned, the wearer knows how to use it.

Its most obvious power is weather control. This seems to be the only one of its powers that Eric actually used. Almost as obvious is the fact that it shouldn't be used too often, nor worn for too long. It drains the wearer of power and strength, because it heightens the wearer's perception. Heightened perception takes energy.

The wearer, in fact, quickly discovers that everything is slowing down around him. The Jewel propels the wearer to the limits of his own existence, destroying all his energies in the process. He will die, unless he surrenders his very existence to the Pattern that is inside the Jewel.

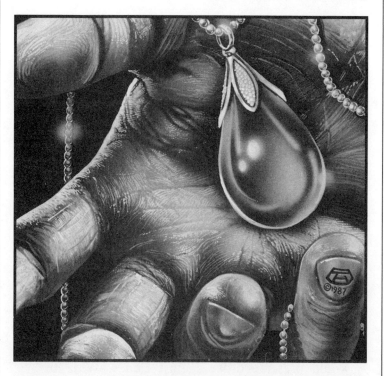

The true Primal Pattern is the one within the Jewel of Judgment. Dworkin fashioned the Pattern from the Jewel, and the Jewel still contains it. For this reason, only the Jewel can repair damage to the Pattern, and only with the aid of the Jewel can a new Pattern be created. But creating a new Pattern, as Corwin and Brand found out, is as mythological an act as Dworkin's creation of the original Pattern. It is as exciting, as beautiful, and as terrifying as all truly primal things.

187

DWORKIN

ive feet tall, hunchbacked, with hair and beard both long and thick, Dworkin is one of the most fascinating of all Amberites. Born in Chaos, he fled there and came to Amber. While in Amber he met and talked with the Unicorn. In a jewel that hung around the Unicorn's neck, the jewel that came to be called the Jewel of Judgment, Dworkin saw a pattern that he felt would preserve order against Chaos. With his blood, he drew the Primal Pattern of Amber. In many ways, therefore, Dworkin and the Pattern are one and the same:

"I am the Pattern, in a very real sense. In passing through my mind to achieve the form it now holds, the foundation of Amber, it marked me as surely as I marked it. I realized one day that I am both the Pattern and myself, and it was forced to become Dworkin in the process of becoming itself. There were mutual modifications in the birthing of this place and this time, and therein lay our weakness as well as our strength. For it occurred to me that damage to the Pattern would be damage to myself, and damage to myself would be reflected within the Pattern. Yet I could not be truly harmed because the Pattern protects me, and who but I could harm the Pattern? A beautiful closed system, it seemed, its weakness totally shielded by its strength."

He was wrong. His blood could deface it. So, as it turned out, could the blood of his offspring. And one of his offspring was Oberon. Thus was born the central conflict that runs throughout Corwin's story. Dworkin is a mythological figure, at least to the average Amberite. Not even the royal family knew he was alive, until by accident he saved Corwin from the dungeon. To most he is incomprehensible and mad, as he works and thinks at the level of the Primal Pattern. To Chaos, from which he fled, he is a Satanic figure, while to Amber he is much closer to God. Yet the mythos of Amber says little about him, except that he was the divine madman who composed *The Book of the Unicorn.* The myths do not reveal that he composed the Pattern as well. By human standards, and even by the standards of the royal family of Amber, Dworkin is insane. But because he is the Pattern, and the Pattern represents Order, Dworkin may well be the most sane mind of all.

REBMA AND TIR-NA NOG'TH

wenty miles south of Kolvir, on the floor of the sea, sits a perfect reflection of Amber itself. A ghost city, Rebma is a mirror-image of Amber, as even its name suggests. Even Amber's Pattern is mirrored, as the Pattern of Rebma shares the original Pattern's powers.

To get to Rebma requires descending Faiella-bionin, the stairway to Rebma. This stairway leads quickly underwater, where air-breathing Amberites can breathe as long as they don't leave the steps. Far down the stairs, a torch shines from a pillar and lights the way to the golden Rebma gates.

The inhabitants of Rebma have hair of green, purple, black, and other colors, and their eyes are green. Their buildings, too, are brightly colored, lit by torches like that which lights the stair. The

pillar-flames continue along a broad avenue to the palace, a perfect image of Castle Amber, where Moire the queen sits upon a throne in a glassite room. Far below the palace, down an even longer set of stairs, lies a duplicate of the Pattern of Amber. This is the Pattern that Corwin walked to restore the memory of his princehood. From the same visit to Rebma came Random's wife Vialle, who has left her home to become Queen of Amber.

Another ghost city reflects Amber's grandeur. At night, rising from the moonlight, Tir-na Nog'th

191

rises high above the peak of Kolvir. It appears in the sky as an insubstantial cloud, then as the moonlight shines through it, and as the observer concentrates upon it, it solidifies into a wavering, accessible form. To get to it from Kolvir requires strength and concentration. It also requires a sane, steady mind.

"I had come to the place where the ghosts play at being ghosts, where the omens, portents, signs, and animate desires thread the nightly avenues and palace high halls of Amber in the sky, Tir-na Nog'th." Corwin's words, frightening and maddening. Later, on the stairway, "If I'd the mind, a few more steps would send me along that celestial escalator into the place of dreams made real, walking neuroses and dubious prophecy, into a moonlit city of ambiguous wish fulfillment, twisted time, and pallid beauty."

Tir-na Nog'th can be accessed only from the Kolvir's highest ridge. There, a formation of stone resembles three steps. If the Amberite is there at the right time, he will see a stairway begin to appear, leading into the sky towards a gleaming, shimmering city. He steps on the stairs and ascends, always being careful not to stare too intently at any one step. If he does, it will lose its opacity and show the terrifying drop to the ground below.

The stairs are long, as long as those leading downwards to Rebma, or those leading up Kolvir

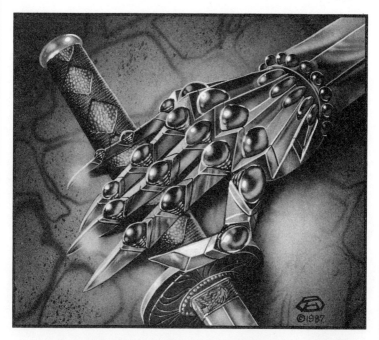

into Amber. The city itself is real, but it *seems* unreal. The palace has a throne, and the throne has a monarch. Everything is distorted, and all seems illusory. The Pattern of Tir-na Nog'th copies the Pattern of Amber, but its colors are different. It is silvery white, without the hint of blue on the original. Because of the effect of Tir-na Nog'th's distortions, this Pattern plays tricks with perspective. Narrowings and widenings seem to shift across its surface, so that an Amberite walking this Pattern would always feel somewhat disoriented. Because of this, walking it is highly dangerous.

193

THE LIGHTHOUSE AT CABRA

n the small, rocky island of Cabra stands a great gray lighthouse. Under the management of Jopin, the old, stooped, bearded keeper, the lighthouse has long guided ships into the port at Amber. A long stone stair leads from a small quay to the door in the lighthouse's western face. Inside, the lighthouse is filled with nautical equipment, maps, whisky, and books. Since Corwin chose Cabra as his destination when he escaped from the dungeon, the lighthouse has become famous. For Jopin, this means more visitors, and he is a man who likes to be alone.

ARDEN FOREST
AND THE HELLHOUNDS

f Amber is the first of all worlds, then Arden is the first of all forests. Stunningly beautiful, the forest bears trees of many kinds, ranging from pines to oaks and through to maples, all of which tower majestically and all of which welcome only the visitors they like. As a youth Corwin spent hours, even days, in the forest, and there is some thought that he is living there now. But the forest is Julian's province, as it has been ever since Eric posted him there shortly before Corwin's return after his lengthy amnesia. In Julian's charge are the Hellhounds, the ghastly, demonic half-wolves that he trained for his own only after he nearly died from their assaults. They are his, but he does not trust them. Like him, they are simply too dangerous.

CULTURE OF
AMBER

THE ARTS

ike all cultures, Amber has its arts and artists. Painting, sculpture, tapestry, dance, music, theater, and literature all have their place, each doing its best to disseminate and reflect the culture as a whole.

As in our own world's Renaissance, there is a rift between the spiritual and the secular in art. During Oberon's rule the spiritual dominated because of Oberon's strong links with the religion of the Unicorn, but since his departure the artists have felt free to experiment and to satirize. The succession to the throne always in doubt, poets and singers began to joke about the possibilities of the next ruler. The songs and stories about Flora were particularly crushing.

The Interregnum — between the reigns of Oberon and Random — also saw more than its share of tragedy. Part of this had to do with the fate of Corwin, but Eric suppressed tragedians from writing of him directly. So they concocted dramas of rulers before Oberon, or of kings far off in Shadow, and at times the allegory was thinly disguised.

At Eric's death, Benedict commissioned several works of art about the event. Two huge paintings now hang in the public theater, and a large tapestry has found its way into the castle. In addition, he commissioned a Tragedy and a Silent Dance (a favorite art form among Amberian nobility). Both are well on their way to the status of classic.

Strangely, Amberian art tends towards the formless rather than the formal. One would think that, with the mythology of the fight against Chaos, art would become highly formal, but instead the reverse has occurred. Drama tends towards improvisation, music towards the absence of chord structures, and even still-life paintings will strive for elements of disorientation.

The model for Amberian art, in fact, seems almost to be the hellride. During Random's reign, in which creativity is encouraged, elements of pure abstraction have begun to appear in the visual arts, and atonality has entered music. A recent drama, furthermore, had two actors sit on the stage for two full hours, neither moving nor speaking. It was called, perhaps inevitably, *A Talk with Two Chaosians.*

This is highbrow stuff, though, and the demands of the masses are somewhat different. In all forms of popular secular art, the carnival is a central element. These arts center around people in celebration, as they sing, drink, laugh, and cry their way through their daily lives. Often, in the visual arts, Castle Amber will appear in the distance, the sun gleaming from its golden sheen. In satiric art, the castle is sometimes upside-down. One infamous canvas, whose artist was never identified, showed Flora and a unicorn in extreme carnal transport. Flora herself ordered it burned.

There is a court-centered literature, dance, and music. Masques and Silent Dances are popular with the royals, and Random has even begun a series of Royal Command Performances. The current Bard of Amber — equivalent to the British Poet Laureate — works with the court jesters on comic poems when he is not working on his epic about Eric's death. There are rumors of an epic poet from a distant Shadow chronicling the story of Corwin, but as yet no poet in Amber has tackled this complex subject.

Religious art continues, but its influence is weakening. Paintings of the Unicorn are always "the right thing to do," while the best artists will even try to depict Oberon in battle. Supposedly, an elderly poet is completing an enormous work about the end of Amber's innocence. He links it to Shadow-shifting, claiming that by learning to travel to Shadows Oberon opened the road to Chaos. But this poet is blind, and likely to die before he finishes. Amber's great literary work is *The Book of the Unicorn.* Reputedly written by Dworkin, after conversation with the Unicorn, this book synthesizes the major myths of ancient Amber, in the same way that Homer describes the myths of ancient Greece. *The Book of the Unicorn* is to Amberian art what *The Iliad*, *The Odyssey*, and the *Bible* are to our own Western art. It is, in other words, the underpinnings of everything.

Inevitably, some art comes in from Shadow. Many of the royal family have brought artwork with them from their travels, and even though they forbid any Amberite from looking at them, descriptions have managed to filter down to the people. These influences likely make Amberian art even more chaotic than it already is.

CRIME
AND PUNISHMENT

he people of Amber are protected by a civil code, a criminal code, and — for the nobility at least — a body of house law. The king is the ultimate authority in legal matters, although an older philosophy gives final say to the Unicorn.

Although the royal family is technically governed by all the legal codes, practically speaking they are above the law. They can be tried for crimes, but none ever has been. There are tales that an Amberian noble tried to bring charges against Oberon for the murder of the noble's wife, but the noble is supposed to have died before the trial took place. Since no record of the accusation exists, however, the story is probably apocryphal.

Because the king is absolute, he cannot be deposed except by force (or abdication). Again practically speaking, the rest of the royal family could get rid of him, but a civil war would likely result. No king has ever been deposed.

Besides civil, criminal, and house laws, a fourth legal option is available. The personal vendetta has been the royal family's method of settling disputes for centuries, and the system has filtered down to the nobility and even further. Among the populace, vendetta to the point of death is technically forbidden, but homicide committed under the blanket of a vendetta is always treated more leniently than regular homicide.

Trials are held only in the case of crimes by the nobility. Non-nobles are dealt with expediently, and if the crime is against a noble, that noble will likely be the punisher. Under Random's rule, public torture is forbidden, but public execution is still fairly common. Lesser punishments range from paying fines to becoming a noble's slave for life.

arious kinds of magic exist within Amber and its surrounding regions. Simple shamanistic magic is practiced by some people, especially those in the less populated areas, while full ritual magic can be found in the cities. Minor magics are ubiquitous, and in fact aren't considered magic at all. The kitchen staff of Castle Amber, for instance, know a spell to keep meat from spoiling. This, however, is the limit of their magical ability.

A considerable amount of magic is attributed to the influence of the Unicorn. Like the dragons and the manticores, the Unicorn is a magical creature, able to traverse Shadow easily and at will. The Unicorn is said to bring with it from Shadow magical energies that allow for the creation of new spells and talents.

Castle Amber itself is protected in part by a system of magical gems that look out from the walls. Activated by the Jewel of Judgment, these gems form a magical defensive shield. Although this shield will not ward off a sustained assault, it will help fill the gaps where defenders have vacated. Naturally, it is most useful in times of siege.

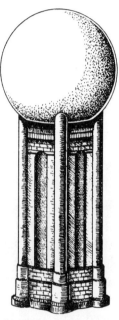

Of course, the royal family are also considered sorcerers. With their abilities to Shadow-shift, to Trump, and to visit the Unicorn and climb to Tir-na Nog'th, they are seen by the average Amberite to be creatures of magic. The mystery surrounding their magical abilities forms part of their reputation as demi-gods.

RELIGION
AND MYTHOLOGY

The Primacy of Amber

ll of Amber's mythology, and all of its religion as well, is based upon the notion that Amber is primary. In some versions of the mythology, Amber is the first Shadow, while in others it casts the first Shadow, and is not a Shadow at all. This difference, between Amber as "first place" and Amber as "first Shadow," has produced a sharp rift between the various religions in the city itself. The only thing preventing religious war through the ages has been the preeminence of the state religion of the Unicorn. In this religion, the Unicorn is the First Cause, and Amber springs from It. This fundamental myth of primacy is the cause of Corwin's enormous surprise at finding a Pattern that controls even the Pattern of Amber. Raised as he was under with the idea that Amber was absolute, the series of events in *Sign of the Unicorn*, *The Hand of Oberon*, and *The Courts of Chaos* upset his long-held notions of what reality was. There's some speculation, in fact, that he disappeared afterwards because he feared for his own sanity.

The War with Chaos

hile Amber sits at one extreme, thinking itself primary, Chaos guards the other, thinking its dominance inevitable. The two conflict always, even if they are not in actual war. At the heart of the conflict is fear. Amber is based on causes: on cause and effect, on order, and on hierarchy and law. Chaos, as its name suggests, is based on the absence of all these. Obviously, Amber and Chaos can't co-exist. Where Amber is strong, Chaos is weak, and the reverse holds true as well. Looked at in the terms of twentieth-century science, Amber sees itself in constant battle against entropy — against the dispersal of energy. Now, the second law of thermodynamics insists that entropy will inevitably take over everything; that's why all ordered systems eventually fail. Amber's mythology, then, is one that guards against this fall. And it fears the spread of Chaos. Probably, that's what the Unicorn is all about. A creature of legend, it comes from a past when Chaos was weak. And legends themselves show a kind of comforting order. What the Unicorn seems to represent is something that denies Chaos.

The Royal Family: Gods, Heroes, Rulers

Most people of Amber see their rulers as both paternalistic and fearsome. The royal family takes excellent care of their subjects — Amber is no democracy — but their mysterious powers are beyond the people's understanding. Add to this the stories of court horror, and the long, unexplained disappearances of some of the royal favorites, and the people's wariness becomes easy to understand.

Corwin, for instance, was gone for many years. So many years, in fact, that many of his most devoted followers died, trying to bequeath their devotion to their children. By the time he reappeared, some of these followers had died, and most of those remaining had already switched loyalties. He even had a tomb, after all. To the royals, Corwin's appearance was either good or inconvenient; to the populace, it was nothing short of miraculous.

The royals do many other strange things as well. They talk into cards, occasionally they disappear into them, they leave for long periods and return

with thoroughly bizarre people and things, they talk of worlds that couldn't possibly exist, and they seem to be beyond even dying.

For all these reasons, the people of Amber see the royal family as not just rulers, but as heroes and gods as well. Officially, they are mortal, but pronouncements of their death are viewed by the people as simply rumors. Their martial exploits make them heroes, especially when they save Amber. And their powers give them an aura of godhood, even though officially they deny it.

211

The Unicorn & The Religion of the Unicorn

eautiful, mysterious, and the subject of rumor after rumor, the Unicorn stands at the forefront of Amberian religion and mythology. The Unicorn is Amber's First Cause, as well as a kind of patron saint. Everything in Amber traces back to the Unicorn, because the Unicorn traces back to the Pattern.

At least, that's the official story. In fact, the Unicorn mythos is relatively recent. Oberon saw the Unicorn, and adopted it as the primary symbol of Amber. Whether or not the rest of the mythos is true doesn't really matter; Oberon's beginnings are themselves part of Amber's system of myths.

At the heart of the Unicorn mythos is *The Book of the Unicorn*. Attributed to Dworkin, it sets out the individual myths. Translations from the ancient Thari can now be found in Amberian temples.

Mythologically, the Unicorn unites Amber. Practically, it forms the basis of the state religion.

The state religion *is* the religion of the Unicorn. Other religions are permitted, but the Unicorn's is official. The religion is far from unified, however; it has many variants, and many denominations.

The variants stem from the way in which an individual temple begins. Basically, temples are the results of Unicorn sightings. Seeing the Unicorn

212

is a miracle, and the person who saw it will help establish a temple at that location. The temples themselves are simply small, open places of worship, and people will choose whose sighting they feel is more important, or in fact which ones to believe.

Priests of the Unicorn conduct temple ceremonies. Their regalia associates them with the location in which the Unicorn was originally sighted, and prayers attempt to return the Unicorn to that location. The claim, of course, is that the Unicorn is there while the ceremony is going on.

Unicorn days (holy days) are associated with each specific temple. There are no national Unicorn days, except for one. On Midsummer's Eve, the people of Amber take to the outdoors in a celebration of feasting, dancing, laughter, and music. It is said that on Midsummer's Night, in the mists of the past, Dworkin spoke with the Unicorn. From their talk he created *The Book of the Unicorn.*

Because the following for each religion is small, no religion — or Unicorn variation — has political clout. This suits the royal family just fine.

FLORA AND FAUNA

ince the city of Amber is cut into the side of the mountain Kolvir, the immediate area is naturally a mountain ecology. Parts of the mountains are dense with trees, while others, especially the higher regions, are more sparse. Water is plentiful from the numerous springs that dot the mountain, but no major rivers trace their source from Kolvir.

The two dominant evergreens resemble the ponderosa pine and the blue spruce of Shadow Earth. In the lower areas live scattered clusters of deciduous trees, but these do not become stately until they reach the inner portions of Arden Forest. In the autumn their leaves turn gold rather than red, and a completely golden tree is said to have a crown of amber. Through the ages, songs and poems have reflected this rather obvious analogy.

Animal species, too, are fairly typical for a mountain environment. But in addition to the unsurprising species, Amber boasts (and sometimes loathes) a host of strange animals. Dragons of various sizes and temperaments exist, although nothing huge and few especially dangerous. There are rumors of a harpylike creature, but few Amberites today even claim to have seen one. On the mountains can be found thick snakes with variously colored feathers, and these are frequently venomous.

Many dangerous beasts exist in Arden Forest. Here can be seen the dire wolves, and here too are tigers with green stripes. Feathery snakes with deadly venom slither among the trees, their colors camouflaging them perfectly. And wingless manticores stalk into the forest at night.

Nor are the cuddlies particularly cuddly. Many a visitor has seen small, rabbit-sized animals with fur of pure white, peacefully feeding on grass or a fallen leaf. Charmed, the visitors carefully step towards them, extend their arms and pick them up. In an instant sharp teeth are injecting venom into their veins, and by the time they shake the creature loose their arms are already numbing. If they're lucky, they will make it to an herbalist. If not, they will die. These creatures aren't numerous, but their reputation is huge.

The most fascinating maritime creature is a manlike fish. It is not a merman, but is rather a nearly developed man with a combination of skin and scales. Largely amphibious (it can't survive for extended periods out of water), it is semi-intelligent. Quite easily tamed, this creature is used to deliver messages and to fight in off-shore sea battles. Random has begun using them as spies.

Amber's two most common animals are the horse and the cat. Horses probably came in from Shadow in eons past, and they are used exclusively for transportation. Cats have a split origin. Many breeds are from Shadow, while some are native Amberian. Cross-breeding has been rampant, though, so by now it's impossible to tell which is which. At times, the cat population reaches a critical stage, and extermination becomes necessary.

Because of the possibility of Shadow-shifting, Amber sees more than its share of weird, one-of-a-kind creatures. In all cases they come in from Shadow, either with an army, in a sorcerer's spell, or on the wings of a Shadow-storm. Some, like the manticore and the Unicorn, are magical, wandering through Shadow at will.

TRADE AND COMMERCE

lthough remarkable in almost all other respects, Amber is quite typical in the field of trade and commerce. It trades most frequently and voluminously with the kingdoms of the Golden Circle; in fact, for them Amber has even drawn up a standard trade treaty.

Amber also trades with neighboring Shadows. Here too, though, the goods exchanged are unremarkable, except for some exotic spices, wines, and cloths. Trade of this kind demands minor Shadow-shifting, which is handled by the equivalent of a minister of trade. This official is trained by the king himself, and his movements are strictly followed.

Amberian professions are those found in any well-to-do city of the late medieval or early Renaissance period on Shadow Earth. The only exceptions are the insanity doctors, who treat mostly people who enter Amber from Shadow unwittingly. They also treat any non-royal who has laid eyes on the Pattern, or who has attempted to climb the stairway to Tir-na Nog'th. Most such cases, however, are untreatable.

There is also a small profession dedicated to the handling and display of exotic and magical creatures. For the most part, though, these creatures are simply left alone.

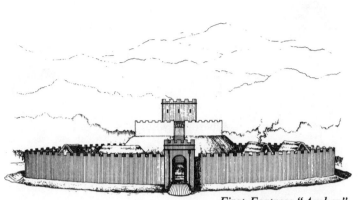

First Fortress "Amber"

When Oberon first established Amber, he faced many enemies. One of his first acts was to construct a motte and bailey fortification. After a few years this grew into a stout, log fortress that survived a number of sieges. It was finally burnt by a Shadow army imported by the Courts, but Oberon rallied his forces and defeated them in a fierce battle.

Original Stone Castle "Amber"

The first true stone castle was built on the same site several centuries ago. The current castle is really just an expansion of this first one, and many of the walls on the first floor date back to the original stone construction.

APPENDIX:
THE FAMILIES OF OBERON

WITH CRESTS AND COLORS

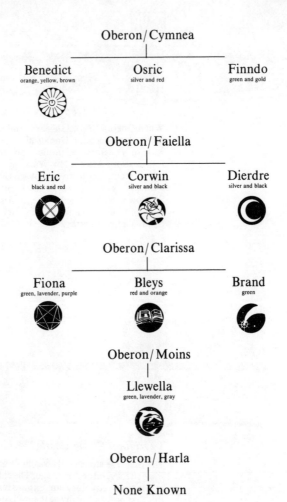

Oberon/Cymnea

Benedict
orange, yellow, brown

Osric
silver and red

Finndo
green and gold

Oberon/Faiella

Eric
black and red

Corwin
silver and black

Dierdre
silver and black

Oberon/Clarissa

Fiona
green, lavender, purple

Bleys
red and orange

Brand
green

Oberon/Moins

Llewella
green, lavender, gray

Oberon/Harla

None Known

Oberon/Rilga

Caine
black and green

Julian
white and black

Gerard
blue and gray

Oberon/Dybele

Flora
green and gray

Oberon/Kinta

Coral

Oberon/Paulette

Random
orange, red, and brown

Mirelle
red and yellow

Oberon/Lora

Sand
pale tan and dark brown

Delwin
brown and black

Oberon/Deela

Dalt
black and green

RETURN TO AMBER...
THE ONE *REAL* WORLD, OF WHICH ALL OTHERS, INCLUDING EARTH, ARE BUT SHADOWS

The Triumphant conclusion of the **Amber** novels

PRINCE OF CHAOS   75502-5/$4.99 US/$5.99 Can

The Classic Amber Series

NINE PRINCES IN AMBER 01430-0/$4.50 US/$5.50 Can
THE GUNS OF AVALON   00083-0/$3.95 US/$4.95 Can
SIGN OF THE UNICORN   00031-9/$3.95 US/$4.95 Can
THE HAND OF OBERON   01664-8/$4.50 US/$5.50 Can
THE COURTS OF CHAOS 47175-2/$4.50 US/$5.50 Can
BLOOD OF AMBER   89636-2/$3.95 US/$4.95 Can
TRUMPS OF DOOM   89635-4/$3.95 US/$4.95 Can
SIGN OF CHAOS   89637-0/$3.95 US/$4.95 Can
KNIGHT OF SHADOWS   75501-7/$3.95 US/$4.95 Can